Feminine KNITS

22 TIMELESS DESIGNS

lene holme samsøe

INTERWEAVE

interweavestore.com

The author would like to thank the sample knitters; Stella Nova, NoaNoa, IC Companys, and La Finesse, which very kindly loaned garments; and Alice Rosendal (www.alicekunst.dk) for the use of the summer house.

First published in 2007 by Aschehoug Dansk Forlag A/S.

TRANSLATION Carol Huebscher Rhoades

EDITOR Anne Merrow

COVER DESIGN Pamela Norman

INTERIOR DESIGN Pam Uhlenkamp

PHOTOGRAPHY Niels Jensen

STYLING & LOCATION Lene Holme Samsøe

MAKE-UP & STYLING Shelley Maris

TECHNICAL EDITORS Rita Greenfeder, Donna Druchunas

TECHNICAL ILLUSTRATION Katherine Jackson

PRODUCTION Katherine Jackson

First North American edition published in 2009 by Interweave Press LLC.

Interweave Press LLC
201 East Fourth Street
Loveland, CO 80537-5655 USA
interweavestore.com

Printed in China by Asia Pacific Offset.

Library of Congress Cataloging-in-Publication Data

Samsøe, Lene Holme.

Feminine knits : 22 timeless designs / Lene Holme Samsøe.

    p. cm.
Includes index.
ISBN 978-1-59668-140-8

    1. Knitting--Patterns. I. Title.

TT825.S25 2009
746.43'2041--dc22

                    2009001064

10 9 8 7 6 5 4 3 2 1

contents

FEMININE KNITTING

To me, feminine knitting means fine patterns and details as well as style. The patterns that follow are designed to be flattering and attractive for women to look their best.

These designs range from lacy and open to cabled and warm and from simple to more embellished. You'll find knit garments for every knitting mood and every occasion. Follow them exactly or incorporate your own style!

With good wishes for your knitting,

Lene Holme Samsøe

CHOOSING THE RIGHT SIZE

Because most of these patterns are designed for a relatively close fit, it is important to compare the finished measurements in each pattern with your own measurements or those from a similar garment that fits well. If you don't want a fitted style, you can choose to omit the waist shaping. (For jackets and other pieces where the front pieces don't meet exactly at the center, the back width measurement is given.)

These patterns were designed for a woman of average height, about 5'4" to 5' 8" (164–172 cm); if you are taller or shorter, you may want to shorten or lengthen the pieces for your height for the most flattering fit, being sure to keep the wait shaping at your waist. If you have longer or shorter arms, knit the sleeves to the right length for you.

FOLLOWING THE PATTERNS

Before you begin knitting, read through the pattern but keep the following general directions in mind.

EDGE STITCHES

Most of the garments in this book include edge stitches (or selvedge stitches) at each edge to be seamed; sew inside the edge stitches when joining the pieces. Work the edge stitches in garter stitch. Work all increases and decreases inside the edge stitches. All increases and decreases (for example, along the side seams) are worked inside the edge stitches.

GAUGE

Always knit a gauge swatch—with the same pattern and needles specified in the pattern—before you start knitting. If you have the same gauge as given in the pattern, you are ready to go! If not, adjust your needle size until you have the correct number of stitches per inch. (The stitch gauge is the most important measurement; when it is correct, the row gauge is generally also correct.) Even a small difference in the gauge from that in the pattern can make a big difference in the size of the finished garment. A sweater that should measure 39½" (100 cm) can wind up 37½" (95 cm) or 41½" (105 cm) if your gauge is 21 sts or 19 sts instead of 20 sts per 4" (10 cm)—making your sweater a full size smaller or larger than you wanted. Don't forget the gauge swatch!

CHARTS

Many knitting patterns are easier to explain with charts than written text; many of the symbols resemble the stitch(es) they represent. For these patterns, the first row of each chart starts on the right side of the fabric. Begin where indicated for your size (or at the lower right-hand corner if no sizes are indicated) and repeat the chart as indicated.

plissé JACKET

This jacket is worked in stripes with two completely different yarns: a thin kid mohair yarn and a wool yarn with a fine glitter thread. The result is a "pleated" effect that looks more complex than it really is.

FINISHED MEASUREMENTS

35½ (37¾, 40¼, 42½)" (90 [96, 102, 108] cm) bust circumference; 19¼ (20, 21, 21¾)" (49 [51, 53, 55] cm) length from CO edge to shoulders.

YARN

DK weight (#3 Light).
Shown here: Coats Løve Opera (86% wool, 9% viscose, 5% polyester; 128 yd [117 m]/50 g): black (wool), 7 (7, 8, 9) balls; and Coats Fonty Kidopale (70% kid mohair, 30% polyamide; 275 yd [250 m]/25 g): black (mohair), 2 (2, 2, 3) balls. See page 126 for yarn substitution suggestions.

NEEDLES

U.S. size 2 (3 mm) and U.S. size 6 (4 mm): straight. U.S. size 2 (3 mm): 24 or 32" (60 or 80 cm) circular (cir). Adjust needle sizes if necessary to obtain the correct gauge.

GAUGE

22 sts and 29 rows = 4" (10 cm) in stockinette stitch on larger needles.

NOTE

Work the first and last stitch of every row in garter stitch (knit on RS and WS).

stitch guide

STRIPE PATTERN
Note: After ribbing, fronts, back, and sleeves are worked in Stripe Pattern throughout.

Rows 1–6: With mohair, work in St st.

Rows 7–12: With wool, work in St st.

BACK

With smaller needles and wool, CO 113 (122, 128, 137) sts.

Beg with a WS row, work ribbing as foll: K2, [p1, k2] to end. Work in patt as established (working sts as they appear and keeping edge sts in garter st) until piece measures 1¼" (3 cm), ending after a RS row.

Next row: (WS) Work in patt and *at the same time* dec 16 (19, 19, 20) sts evenly across row as foll: K2, *p1, k2, p1, k2tog; rep from * 15 (18, 18, 19) more times, work in patt to end of row—97 (103, 109, 117) sts rem.

Change to larger needles and work Stripe Pattern until piece measures 2 (3¼, 4¼, 5½)" (5 [8, 11, 14] cm) from CO.

Cont in patt and *at the same time* k2tog one st from each edge every RS row 4 times—89 (95, 101, 109) sts rem.

Cont even in patt until piece measures 7 (8¼, 9½, 10¾)" (18 [21, 24, 27] cm) from CO.

Cont in patt and *at the same time* k1f&b one st from each edge every RS row 4 times—97 (103, 109, 117) sts.

Work even in Stripe Pattern until piece measures 11¾ (12¼, 12½, 13)" (30 [31, 32, 33] cm) from CO.

SHAPE ARMHOLE
BO 3 sts at beg of next 2 (2, 4, 4) rows, 2 sts at beg of next 4 (4, 2, 4) rows, 1 st at beg of next 6 (8, 8, 6) rows for armhole shaping—77 (81, 85, 91) sts rem.

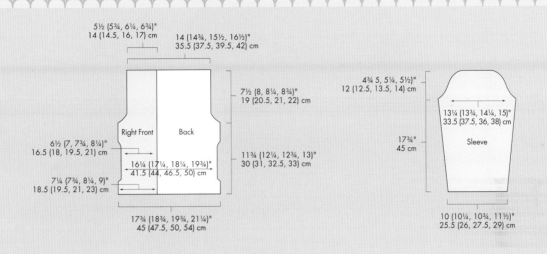

5½ (5¾, 6¼, 6¾)"
14 (14.5, 16, 17) cm

14 (14¾, 15½, 16½)"
35.5 (37.5, 39.5, 42) cm

7½ (8, 8¼, 8¾)"
19 (20.5, 21, 22) cm

Right Front Back

6½ (7, 7¾, 8¼)"
16.5 (18, 19.5, 21) cm

16¼ (17¼, 18¼, 19¾)"
41.5 (44, 46.5, 50) cm

11¾ (12¼, 12¾, 13)"
30 (31, 32.5, 33) cm

7¼ (7¾, 8¼, 9)"
18.5 (19.5, 21, 23) cm

17¾ (18¾, 19¾, 21¼)"
45 (47.5, 50, 54) cm

4¾ 5, 5¼, 5½)"
12 (12.5, 13.5, 14) cm

13¼ (13¾, 14¼, 15)"
33.5 (37.5, 36, 38) cm

17¾"
45 cm

Sleeve

10 (10¼, 10¾, 11½)"
25.5 (26, 27.5, 29) cm

Cont even in patt until armhole measures 7½ (7¾, 8¼, 8¾)" (19 [20, 21, 22] cm) from beg of armhole shaping. Place rem sts on a holder for collar.

LEFT FRONT

With smaller needles and wool, CO 47 (50, 53, 59) sts. Work ribbing as for back until piece measures 1¼" (3 cm), ending after a RS row.

NEXT ROW: (WS) Work in patt and *at the same time* dec 7 (7, 7, 9) sts evenly across row as foll: K2, *p1, k2, p1, k2tog; rep from * 6 (6, 6, 8) more times, work in patt to end of row—40 (43, 46, 50) sts rem.

Change to larger needles and work in Stripe Pattern until piece measures 2 (3¼, 4¼, 5½)" (5 [8, 11, 14] cm) from CO.

Cont in patt and *at the same time* k2tog one st from side edge (beg of RS rows) every RS row 4 times—36 (39, 42, 46) sts rem.

Cont even in patt until piece measures 7 (8¼, 9½, 10¾)" (18 [21, 24, 27] cm) from CO.

Cont in patt and *at the same time* k1f&b one st from each edge 4 times—40 (43, 46, 50) sts. Work even in Stripe Pattern until piece measures 11¾ (12¼, 12½, 13)" (30 [31, 32, 33] cm) from CO.

SHAPE ARMHOLE
BO at armhole edge at beg of every other row: 3 sts 1 (1, 2, 2) time(s), 2 sts 2 (2, 1, 2) time(s), 1 st 3 (4, 4,

3) times—30 (32, 34, 37) sts rem.

Work even in patt until armhole measures 7½ (7¾, 8¼, 8¾)" (19 [20, 21, 22] cm) from beg of armhole shaping. Place rem sts on a holder for collar.

RIGHT FRONT

With smaller needles and wool, CO 47 (50, 53, 59) sts. Work ribbing as for back until piece measures 1¼" (3 cm), ending after a RS row.

NEXT ROW: (WS) Work in patt and *at the same time* dec 7 (7, 7, 9) sts evenly across row as foll: K2, *p1, k2, p1, k2tog; rep from * 6 (6, 6, 8) more times, work in patt to end of row—40 (43, 46, 50) sts rem.

Change to larger needles and work in Stripe Pattern until piece measures 2 (3¼, 4¼, 5½)" (5 [8, 11, 14] cm) from CO.

Cont in patt and *at the same time* k2tog one st from side edge (end of RS rows) every RS row 4 times—36 (39, 42, 46) sts rem.

Cont even in patt until piece measures 7 (8¼, 9½, 10¾)" (18 [21, 24, 27] cm) from CO.

Cont in patt and *at the same time* k1f&b one st from side edge 4 times—40 (43, 46, 50) sts. Work even in Stripe Pattern until piece measures 11¾ (12¼, 12½, 13)" (30 [31, 32, 33] cm) from CO.

SHAPE ARMHOLE
BO at armhole edge at beg of every other row: 3 sts 1 (1, 2, 2) time(s), 2 sts 2 (2, 1, 2) times, 1 st 3 (4, 4, 3) times—30 (32, 34, 37) sts rem.

Work even in patt until armhole measures 7½ (7¾, 8¼, 8¾)" (19 [20, 21, 22] cm) from beg of armhole shaping. Place rem sts on a holder for collar.

SLEEVES
With smaller needles and wool, CO 62 (65, 68, 71) sts. Work ribbing as for back until piece measures 1¼"

(3 cm), ending after a RS row.
NEXT ROW: (WS) Work in patt and *at the same time* dec 7 (8, 9, 8) sts evenly across row as foll: K2, p1, k2, *p1, k2, p1, k2tog; rep from * 6 (7, 8, 7) more times, work in patt to end of row—55 (57, 59, 63) sts rem.

Change to larger needles. Work in Stripe Pattern and *at the same time* k1f&b one st from each edge after the first (first, second, second) stripe as foll:

*Working in patt, k1f&b one st from each edge.

Work 11 rows even in patt.

Rep from * 8 (8, 9, 9) more times—73 (75, 79, 83) sts.

Cont even in patt until piece measures 17¾" (45 cm) from CO, ending at the same place in Stripe Pattern as for beginning of armhole on back.

SHAPE CAP

BO 3 sts at beg of next 2 rows, 2 (2, 3, 3) sts at beg of next 2 rows, 2 sts at beg of next 2 rows, then 1 st at beg of next 12 (14, 16, 18) rows. BO 2 sts at beg of next 10 rows, then 3 sts at beg of next 6 rows. BO rem 9 (9, 9, 11) sts.

FINISHING

SHOULDERS

Place held 30 (32, 34, 37) right front sts, 77 (81, 85, 91) back sts, and 30 (32, 34, 37) left front sts on larger needles—137 (145, 153, 165) sts. Cont in Stripe Pattern, work even for 2¾" (7 cm), ending with a mohair stripe after a WS row.

NEXT ROW: Work in patt and *at the same time* inc 15 (16, 17, 14) sts evenly across row as M1 (see Glossary)—152 (161, 170, 179) sts.

COLLAR

Change to wool and smaller cir and work back and forth in ribbing.

Beg with a WS row, work ribbing as foll: K2, [p1, k2] to end. Work in patt as established (working sts as they appear) for 3¼" (8 cm). BO in ribbing.

FRONT EDGING

With RS facing, using smaller cir and wool, pick up and knit 158 (161, 164, 167) sts (making sure to have a multiple of 3 sts plus 2) along one front edge. Beg with a WS row, work ribbing as foll: K2, [p1, k2] to end. Work in patt as established (working sts as they appear) for 3¼" (8.5 cm). BO all sts in ribbing. Rep for other front edge.

With yarn threaded on a tapestry needle, use invisible method (see Glossary) to sew in sleeves, then sew sleeve underarms and side seams, being careful to match up stripes. Weave in ends.

surplice
SWEATER

The V neckline and wrap style of this top provide a flattering shape for every figure. The wrap look is an illusion; the sweater is joined at the sides. The crocheted edging is a fine detail on this otherwise totally classic top.

FINISHED MEASUREMENTS
34¾ (37, 39½, 41¾)" (88 [94, 100, 106] cm) bust circumference; 21¼ (22, 22¾, 23¾)" (54 [56, 58, 60] cm) length from CO edge to shoulders.

YARN
DK weight (Light #3).
Shown here: Sandnes Alpakka (100% alpaca; 66 yd [60 m]/50 g): #6063 blue, 9 (9, 10, 11) balls. See page 126 for yarn substitution suggestions.

NEEDLES
U.S. size 2 (3 mm) and U.S. size 6 (4 mm): straight. U.S. size D (3 mm) crochet hook. Adjust needle sizes if necessary to obtain the correct gauge.

GAUGE
22 sts and 29 rows = 4" (10 cm) in stockinette stitch on larger needles.

NOTE
Work the first and last stitch of every row in garter stitch (knit on RS and WS).

stitch guide

CROCHET PICOT
Ch 3, 1 sc in first ch.

BACK

With smaller needles, CO 98 (106, 110, 118) sts.

Beg with a WS row, work ribbing as foll: K1, p1, [k2, p2] to last 4 sts, k2, p1, k1. Work in patt as established (working sts as they appear and maintaining garter st edges) until piece measures 4¾" (12 cm), ending after a WS row.

NEXT ROW: (RS) Inc 1 (dec 1, inc 2, inc 1) st(s) evenly across row—99 (105, 112, 119) sts.

Change to larger needles and work in St st until piece measures 5½" (14 cm) from CO, ending after a WS row.

*NEXT ROW: (RS; dec row) K1, k2tog, knit to last until 3 sts, ssk, k1. Work even for 5 rows. Rep from * 2 more times—93 (99, 106, 113) sts rem.

Work even until piece measures 8¾ (9¾, 10¾, 12¾)" (22 [27, 25, 32] cm) from CO.

*NEXT ROW: (RS; inc row) K1, k1f&b, knit to last 2 sts, k1f&b, k1. Work even for 5 rows.

Rep from * 2 more times—99 (105, 112, 119) sts. Work even until piece measures 13½ (13¾, 14¼, 14½)" (34 [35, 36, 37] cm) from CO, ending after a WS row.

SHAPE ARMHOLES

BO 3 sts at beg of next 2 (2, 4, 4) rows, 2 sts at beg of next 4 (4, 2, 6) rows, 1 st at beg of next 8 (10, 10, 8) rows—77 (81, 86, 87) sts rem.

SHAPE NECK

Work even until armholes measure 7½ (7¾, 8¼, 8¾)" (19 [20, 21, 22] cm), ending after a WS row.

NEXT ROW: (RS) K19 (21, 23, 23), join another ball of yarn and BO center 39 (39, 40, 41) sts, k19 (21, 23, 23).

Working each side separately, BO at beg of each shoulder edge 6 (7, 7, 7) sts once, 6 (7, 8, 8) sts once, then 7 (7, 8, 8) sts once.

RIGHT FRONT

(OUTSIDE PIECE)

Work as for back until piece measures 7 (7, 7½, 8)" (18 [18, 19, 20] cm)—93 (99, 106, 113) sts.

FRONT EDGE

Shape front edge as foll: BO 2 sts at beg of next 16 (17, 18, 20) RS rows and *at the same time* when piece measures 8¾ (9¾, 10¾, 12¾)" (22 [27, 25, 32] cm), k1f&b one

st in from side seam (end of RS rows) next row, then every sixth row twice—64 (68, 73, 76) sts rem. Work 1 row even.

NEXT ROW: (RS) K1, k2tog, knit to end.

NEXT ROW: Work even in patt.

Rep last 2 rows 33 (34, 36, 36) times more and *at the same time* when at same length as back to armhole, BO at armhole edge (beg of WS rows) 3 sts 1 (1, 2, 2) time(s), 2 sts 2 (2, 1, 3) time(s), 1 st 4 (5, 5, 4) times—19 (21, 23, 23) sts rem.

When armhole measures same length as back, BO at shoulder edge 6 (7, 7, 7) sts once, 6 (7, 8, 8) sts once, then 7 (7, 8, 8) sts once.

LEFT FRONT

(INSIDE PIECE)

With larger needles, pick up and knit (see Glossary) 99 (105, 112, 119) sts on WS of the front directly above ribbing by picking up 1 st in the purl bump of every st in the first St st row. Work waist decs as for back—93 (99, 106, 113) sts rem.

FRONT EDGE

Shape front edge as foll: BO 2 sts at beg of next 16 (17, 18, 20) WS rows and *at the same time* when piece measures 8¾ (9¾, 10¾, 12¾)" (22 [27, 25, 32] cm), k1f&b one st in from side seam (beg of RS row) next row then every sixth row twice—64 (68, 73, 76) sts rem. Work 1 row even.

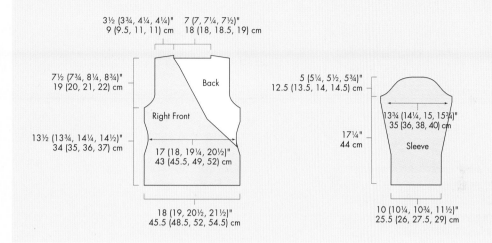

3½ (3¾, 4¼, 4¼)"
9 (9.5, 11, 11) cm

7 (7, 7¼, 7½)"
18 (18, 18.5, 19) cm

7½ (7¾, 8¼, 8¾)"
19 (20, 21, 22) cm

Back

Right Front

5 (5¼, 5½, 5¾)"
12.5 (13.5, 14, 14.5) cm

13¾ (14¼, 15, 15¾)"
35 (36, 38, 40) cm

17¼"
44 cm

Sleeve

13½ (13¾, 14¼, 14½)"
34 (35, 36, 37) cm

17 (18, 19¼, 20½)"
43 (45.5, 49, 52) cm

18 (19, 20½, 21½)"
45.5 (48.5, 52, 54.5) cm

10 (10¼, 10¾, 11½)"
25.5 (26, 27.5, 29) cm

NEXT ROW: (RS) Knit to last 3 sts, ssk, k1.

NEXT ROW: Work even in patt. Rep last 2 rows 33 (34, 36, 36) more times and *at the same time* when at same length as back to armhole, BO at beg of armhole edge 3 sts 1 (1, 2, 2) time(s), 2 sts 2 (2, 1, 3) time(s), 1 st 4 (5, 5, 4) times—19 (21, 23, 23) sts rem. When at same length as back, BO at shoulder edge 6 (7, 7, 7) sts once, 6 (7, 8, 8) sts once, then 7 (7, 8, 8) sts once.

SLEEVES

With smaller needles, CO 58 (62, 62, 66) sts. Work in ribbing as for back for 4¾" (12 cm), ending after a WS row.

NEXT ROW: (RS) With larger needles, work in St st and *at the same time* dec 3 (5, 3, 3) sts evenly across row—55 (57, 59, 63) sts rem.

Cont even in St st until piece

measures 5½" (14 cm), ending after a WS row.

*NEXT ROW: (RS; inc row) K1, k1f&b in next st, knit to last 2 sts, k1f&b, k1.

Work 7 rows even.

Rep from * 9 (10, 11, 11) more times—75 (79, 83, 87) sts. Work even until sleeve measures 17¼" (44 cm) or desired length from CO.

SHAPE CAP

BO 3 sts at beg of next 2 (2, 4, 4) rows, 2 sts at beg of next 4 (4, 2, 4) rows, 1 st at beg of next 14 (16, 18, 18) rows, 2 sts at beg of next 10 rows, and 3 sts at beg of next 6 rows. BO rem 9 (11, 11, 11) sts.

FINISHING

Block to measurements. With yarn threaded on a tapestry needle, use the invisible horizontal seam (see Glossary) to sew shoulder seams.

EDGING

With crochet hook, RS facing, and beginning at right front lower neck edge, work a row of single crochet along the right front neck edge, back neck and left front neck edge working about 17 sc sts for every 4" (10 cm); work more or fewer sc sts if necessary so that the edge lies flat without gathers or ruffles. (See Glossary for crochet directions.) Turn and work another row of sc back, increasing or decreasing as necessary for a multiple of 6 sts. Turn and work a row of picot shells (see Stitch Guide) as foll: *1 dc in the 3rd sc from hook, 1 picot, [1 dc in the same st as previous st, 1 picot] 4 times, skip 2 sc, and 1 sc in next st; rep from * to end. Fasten off.

With yarn threaded on a tapestry needle, use invisible seams (see Glossary) to sew in sleeves, sew sleeve underarms, and sew side seams. Weave in ends.

TOP WITH
pompon ties

The stitch pattern for this sparkly top is just a little lacy; the finished sweater can be worn by itself or with a shirt underneath. In addition to deep ribbing and figure-flattering waist shaping, the drawstring waist is accented with two fun pompons.

FINISHED MEASUREMENTS

35½ (37¾, 40¼, 42½)" (90 [96, 102, 108] cm) bust circumference, 22 (22¾, 23¾, 24½)" (56 [58, 60, 62] cm) length from CO to shoulder edge.

YARN

DK weight (Light #3).
Shown here: Coats Løve Opera (86% wool, 9% viscose, 5% polyester; 128 yd [117 m]/ 50 g): #83 lilac, 8 (8, 9, 10) balls. See page 126 for yarn substitution suggestions.

NEEDLES

U.S. size 2 (3 mm) and U.S. size 6 (4 mm): straight. U.S. size 2 (3 mm): 16" (40 cm) circular (cir). U.S. size 6 (4 mm): 2 double-pointed (dpn). Adjust needle sizes if necessary to obtain the correct gauge.

NOTIONS

Tapestry needle; pompon maker.

GAUGE

22 sts and 29 rows = 4" (10 cm) in stockinette stitch and pattern stitch on larger needles.

NOTE

Work the first and last stitch of every row in garter stitch (knit on RS and WS).

BACK

With smaller straight needles, CO 113 (121, 129, 137) sts.

Beg with a WS row, work ribbing as foll: K2, [p1, k3] to last 3 sts, p1, k2.

Work in patt as established (working sts as they appear and maintaining garter st edges) until piece measures 2" (5 cm), ending after a RS row.

Next row: (WS) K2, p1, k3, *p1, k3, p1, k2tog, k1; rep from * to last 3 sts, p1, k2—100 (107, 114, 121) sts rem.

Work even in patt until piece measures 4" (10 cm), ending after a RS row.

Next row: (WS; dec row) K2, p1, k3, *p1, k2tog, k1, p1, k2; rep from * to last 3 sts, p1, k2—87 (93, 99, 105) sts rem.

Work even in patt until piece measures 5½" (14 cm), ending after a WS row.

With larger straight needles, work Rows 1 and 2 of Pompon chart as indicated for size, working the first and last st of every row in garter st

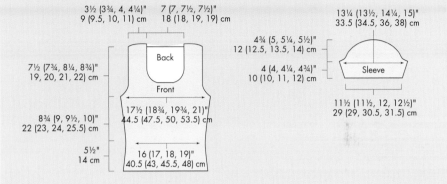

3½ (3¾, 4, 4¼)"
9 (9.5, 10, 11) cm

7 (7, 7½, 7½)"
18 (18, 19, 19) cm

13¼ (13½, 14¼, 15)"
33.5 (34.5, 36, 38) cm

7½ (7¾, 8¼, 8¾)"
19, 20, 21, 22) cm

Back

4¾ (5, 5¼, 5½)"
12 (12.5, 13.5, 14) cm

Front

4 (4, 4¼, 4¾)"
10 (10, 11, 12) cm

Sleeve

8¾ (9, 9½, 10)"
22 (23, 24, 25.5) cm

17½ (18¾, 19¾, 21)"
44.5 (47.5, 50, 53.5) cm

11½ (11½, 12, 12½)"
29 (29, 30.5, 31.5) cm

5½"
14 cm

16 (17, 18, 19)"
40.5 (43, 45.5, 48) cm

(not shown on chart), then rep Rows 3–22 until piece measures 7" (18 cm), ending after a WS row.

Next row: (RS; inc row) K1, M1 (see Glossary) work in patt to last st, M1, k1—89 (95, 101, 107) sts.

Note: Work incs into patt on this row and subsequent inc rows.

Work even in patt until piece measures 8¾" (22 cm), ending after a WS row. Rep inc row—91 (97, 103, 109) sts.

Work even in patt until piece measures 10¼" (26 cm), ending after a WS row. Rep inc row—93 (99, 105, 111) sts.

Work even in patt until piece measures 11¾" (30 cm), ending after a WS row. Rep inc row—95 (101, 107, 113) sts.

Work even in patt until piece measures 13½" (34 cm), ending after a WS row. Rep inc row—97

(103, 109, 115) sts. Work even in patt until piece measures 14¼ (14½, 15, 15½)" (36 [37, 38, 39] cm) from CO.

SHAPE ARMHOLE

BO 3 (3, 3, 3) sts at beg of next 2 (2, 4, 4) rows, 2 sts at beg of next 4 (4, 2, 4) rows, 1 st at beg of next 6 (8, 8, 6) rows—77 (81, 85, 89) sts rem.

Work even in patt until piece measures 7½ (7¾, 8¼, 8¾)" (19 [20, 21, 22] cm) from beg of armhole shaping, ending with a WS row.

SHAPE NECK AND SHOULDERS

Next row: K19 (21, 22, 24), join another ball of yarn and BO center 39 (39, 41, 41) sts, k19 (21, 22, 24).

Working each side separately, BO at beg of each shoulder edge 6 (7, 7, 8) sts once, 6 (7, 7, 8) sts once, then 7 (7, 8, 8) sts once.

FRONT

Work as for back until armhole measures 2½ (2¾, 3¼, 3½)" (6 [7, 8, 9] cm)—77 (81, 85, 89) sts.

SHAPE NECK AND SHOULDERS

Next row: K29 (31, 32, 34), join another ball of yarn and BO center 19 (19, 21, 21) sts, k29 (31, 32, 34).

Working each side separately, BO 3 sts at each neck edge once, 2 sts twice, then 1 st 3 times—19 (21, 22, 24) sts rem each side.

Work until armholes measure 7½ (7¾, 8¼, 8¾)" [19 [20, 21, 22] cm), ending with a WS row. BO shoulder sts as for back.

SLEEVES

With smaller straight needles, CO 68 (71, 74, 77) sts.

Beg with a WS row, work in ribbing as foll: K2, [p1, k2] to end.

POMPON

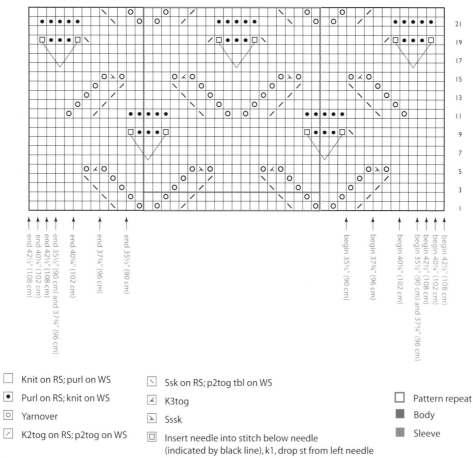

21
19
17
15
13
11
9
7
5
3
1

end 42½" (108 cm)
end 40¼" (102 cm)
end 42½" (108 cm)
end 40¼" (102 cm)
end 35½" (90 cm) and 37¾" (96 cm)
end 37¾" (96 cm)
end 35½" (90 cm)

begin 35½" (90 cm)
begin 37¾" (96 cm)
begin 40¼" (102 cm)
begin 35½" (90 cm) and 37¾" (96 cm)
begin 42½" (108 cm)
begin 40¼" (102 cm)
begin 42½" (108 cm)

☐ Knit on RS; purl on WS	╲ Ssk on RS; p2tog tbl on WS
• Purl on RS; knit on WS	⊼ K3tog
☐ Yarnover	⋏ Sssk
╱ K2tog on RS; p2tog on WS	☐ Insert needle into stitch below needle (indicated by black line), k1, drop st from left needle

☐ Pattern repeat
▪ Body
▪ Sleeve

Work in patt as established (working sts as they appear) until piece measures 1¼" (3 cm), ending after WS row.

NEXT ROW: (RS; dec row) Work in patt as established and *at the same time* dec 5 (8, 7, 8) sts evenly across the knit sts of row—63 (63, 67, 69) sts.

NEXT ROW: (WS) Work in patt as established.

Change to larger straight needles. Working first and last sts of every row in garter st (not shown on chart), work Rows 1–4 of Pattern chart as indicated for Sleeves.

NEXT ROW: (RS; inc row) Keeping in patt, k1, k1f&b, work in patt to last 2 sts, k1f&b, k1.

Rep inc row every 4th row 4 (5, 5, 6) more times, working new sts into patt—73 (75, 79, 83) sts.

Work even in patt until piece measures 4 (4, 4¼, 4¾)" (10 [10, 11, 12] cm), ending after a WS row.

SHAPE SLEEVE CAP

BO 3 sts at beg of next 2 (2, 4, 4) rows and 2 sts at beg of next 4 (4, 2, 2) rows—59 (61, 63, 67) sts rem.

NEXT ROW: (RS; dec row) K1, k2tog, work in patt to last 2 sts, ssk, k1. Rep dec row every other row 5 (6, 7, 8) more times—47 (47, 47, 49) sts rem.

BO 2 sts at beg of next 10 rows, then 3 sts at beg of next 6 rows. BO off rem 9 (9, 9, 11) sts.

FINISHING

Block to measurements. With yarn threaded on a tapestry needle, use invisible horizontal method (see Glossary) to sew shoulder seams.

With smaller cir, pick up and knit (see Glossary) 150 (150, 156, 156) sts around neck edge. Join for working in the round and work k1, p2 ribbing until collar measures for 1¼" (3 cm). BO sts in patt.

Sew in sleeves, then sew underarm and side seams, matching up patt.

I-CORD TIE

With larger dpn, CO 4 sts. Work I-cord (see Glossary) until piece measures 49¼ (51¼, 53, 55¼)" (125 [130, 135, 140] cm). K4tog, cut yarn, and fasten off. Thread tie through lower edge of sweater between ribbing and patt as shown.

Make two 1½" (4 cm) pompons (see Glossary) and sew securely to each end of I-cord.

chevron
TANK

The lacy chevron stitch pattern blends four colors beautifully, with columns of yarnovers drawing the eye vertically. The garter-stitch edging and straps create a polished look for the tank, and the button-accented front creates a flirty finish.

FINISHED SIZE
30 (32¼, 34¾, 36¾)" (76 [82, 88, 93] cm) bust circumference; 13 (13¾, 14½, 15½)" (33 [35, 37, 39] cm) side seam length.

YARN
DK weight (Light #3).
Shown here: Coats Løve Siesta (50% acrylic, 50% viscose; 126 yd [115 m]/50 g): #32 beige, 2 balls; #224 coral, #26 ochre, and #66 aqua, 1 ball each. See page 126 for yarn substitution suggestions.

NEEDLES
U.S. size 2 (3 mm) and U.S. size 4 (3.5 mm): straight. U.S. size 2 (3 mm): 16" (40 cm) circular (cir). Adjust needle size if necessary to obtain the correct gauge.

NOTIONS
Tapestry needle; three ½" (1.3 cm) buttons; sewing needle and matching thread.

GAUGE
24 sts and 31 rows = 4" (10 cm) in patt on larger needles.

NOTE
Work the first and last stitch of every row in garter stitch (knit on RS and WS).

CHEVRON

(chart)

☐	Knit on RS; purl on WS
•	Purl on RS; knit on WS
O	Yarnover
╱	K2tog on RS; p2tog on WS
╲	Ssk on RS; p2tog tbl on WS
☐	Pattern repeat

Chart row numbers: 7, 5, 3, 1

end 32¼", 36¾" end 30", 34"   begin 30", 34" begin 32¼", 36¾"

stitch guide

STRIPE PATTERN
*Work 4 rows beige.
Work 4 rows coral.
Work 4 rows aqua.
Work 4 rows ochre.
Rep from * for patt.

FRONT

With larger needles and beige, CO 94 (100, 107, 113) sts. Knit 1 row.

Working in Stripe patt (see Stitch Guide), work Rows 1–4 of Chevron chart, working the first and last sts in garter st (not shown on chart).

*Cont in Stripe patt, work Rows 5–8 of Chevron chart. Rep from * until piece measures 10¼ (11, 12, 12¾)" (26, 28, 30, 32] cm), ending after a WS row.

SHAPE ARMHOLE
Note: If there are not enough sts to work a dec or yo as given in chart, omit the corresponding yo or dec to maintain st count.

Cont to rep Stripe patt and Rows 5–8 of Chevron chart and *at the same time* BO 3 sts at beg of next 2 rows, 2 sts at beg of next 2 rows—84 (90, 97, 103) sts rem.

NEXT ROW: (RS; dec row) K1, k2tog, work even in patt until 3 sts rem, ssk, k1.

Rep dec row every other row 9 (9, 10, 10) more times—64 (70, 75, 81) sts rem. If necessary, work even in patt to complete stripe.

NEXT ROW: (RS) With smaller needles and beige, knit 1 row and *at the same time* [k3 (3, 4, 4), k2tog] 12 times, work to end of row—52 (58, 63, 69) sts rem.

Knit 3 rows with beige. BO all sts.

BACK

Work as for front through last dec for armhole shaping. Work even, maintaining stripe patt, for 2" (5 cm) more, ending with a complete stripe—64 (70, 75, 81) sts rem.

NEXT ROW: (RS) With smaller needles and beige, knit 1 row and *at the same*

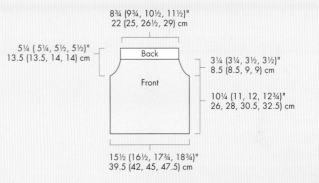

8¾ (9¾, 10½, 11½)"
22 (25, 26½, 29) cm

5¼ (5¼, 5½, 5½)"
13.5 (13.5, 14, 14) cm

Back

Front

3¼ (3¼, 3½, 3½)"
8.5 (8.5, 9, 9) cm

10¼ (11, 12, 12¾)"
26, 28, 30.5, 32.5) cm

15½ (16½, 17¾, 18¾)"
39.5 (42, 45, 47.5) cm

time [k3 (3, 4, 4), k2tog] 12 times, work to end of row—52 (58, 63, 69) sts rem.
Knit 3 rows with beige. BO all sts.

FINISHING

With yarn threaded on a tapestry needle, use invisible vertical seam (see Glossary) to sew side seams.

With smaller cir and beige, and starting at right armhole on upper back, pick up and knit (see Glossary) 1 st in every row along right armhole edge, then CO 74 (78, 82, 84) sts for right shoulder strap. Knit 5 rows. BO all sts.

With smaller cir and beige, CO 74 (78, 82, 84) sts for left shoulder strap, then starting at left armhole at upper back, pick up and knit 1 st in every row along left armhole edge. Knit 5 rows. BO all sts.

Position straps at back, adjusting length to fit. With sewing needle and thread, sew each strap to back and sew 1 button at each join. With yarn threaded on a tapestry needle, using a running stitch (see Glossary) at center front from top to about 10 rows from bound-off neck edge; pull tight to gather. Attach remaining button to top of gather and fasten off thread.

chevron tank

short JACKET
LONG *jacket*

These two jackets, the short one on page 33 and long one opposite, are made with the same basic pattern. You can choose your own variation and make a short jacket with long sleeves or vice versa. The edges of the two jackets are slightly different for variety.

short one on page 33

FINISHED MEASUREMENTS

36½ (38½, 41, 43½)" (92.5 [98, 104, 110.5] cm) bust circumference for both jackets, measured closed; 16½ (17¼, 18¼, 19)" (42 [44, 46, 48] cm) from CO to shoulder edge of short jacket; 22¾ (23¾, 24½, 25¼)" (58 [60, 62, 64] cm) from CO to shoulder edge of long jacket.

YARN

Worsted weight (Medium #4).
Shown here: SHORT JACKET: Coats HP Løve Zeta (100% silk; 104 yd [95 m]/50 g): #26 ochre, 6 (7, 8, 9) balls; LONG JACKET: Coats HP Løve Rustico (55% acrylic, 45% cotton; 109 yd [100 m]/50 g): #32 camel, 9 (10, 11, 12) balls. See page 126 for yarn substitution suggestions.

NEEDLES

SHORT JACKET: U.S. size 8 (5 mm) and U.S. size H/8 (5 mm) crochet hook.

LONG JACKET: U.S. size 10 (6 mm), U.S. size 8 (5 mm), and U.S. size J/10 (6 mm) crochet hook. Adjust needle sizes if necessary to obtain the correct gauge.

NOTIONS

Tapestry needle.

GAUGE

SHORT JACKET: 16 sts and 24 rows = 4" (10 cm) in stockinette st with Zeta and size 8 (5 mm) needles. LONG JACKET: 16 sts and 24 rows = 4" (10 cm) in stockinette st with Rustico and size 10 (6 mm) needles.
Note: Although needle sizes are different, both yarns should be worked at the same gauge.

NOTE

Work the first and last stitch of every row in garter stitch (knit on RS and WS).

BACK

SHORT JACKET

CO 73 (83, 83, 93) sts loosely.

Working first and last sts of each row in garter st (not shown in chart), work Short Jacket Chart A over all sts.

After completing charted pattern, work in St st until piece measures 4¼" (11 cm), ending after a WS row.

NEXT ROW: (RS; dec row) K1, k2tog, knit to last 3 sts, ssk, k1—71 (81, 81, 91) sts rem.

Work even in St st until piece measures 5¼" (13 cm), ending after a WS row.

NEXT ROW: (RS; dec row) K1, k2tog 0 (1, 0, 1) time(s), work in St st to last 1 (3, 1, 3) st(s), ssk 0 (1, 0, 1) time(s), k1—71 (79, 81, 89) sts rem.

Work even until piece measures 6¼ (6¼, 6¾, 6¾)" (16 [16, 17, 17] cm), ending after a WS row.

NEXT ROW: (RS; inc row) K1, k1f&b 1 (0, 1, 0) time(s), knit to last 1 (2, 1, 2) st(s), k1f&b 1 (0, 1, 0) time(s), k1—71 (81, 81, 91) sts.

Work even until piece measures 7½ (7½, 8, 8)" (19 [19, 20, 20] cm), ending after a WS row.

NEXT ROW: (RS; inc row) K1, k1f&b, knit to last 2 sts, k1f&b, k1—73 (83, 83, 93) sts.

Work even in St st until piece measures 8¾ (9, 9½, 9¾)" (22 [23, 24, 25] cm).

LONG JACKET

With larger needles, CO 73 (83, 83, 93) sts loosely.

Working first and last sts of each row in garter st (not shown in chart), work Long Jacket Chart A1 (A, A, A1) over all sts.

After completing charted pattern, work in St st until piece measures 6¼ (6¼, 6¾, 6¾)" (16 [16, 17, 17] cm), ending after a WS row.

NEXT ROW: (RS; dec row) K1, k2tog, knit to last 3 sts, ssk, k1—71 (81, 81, 91) sts rem.

Work even until piece measures 8 (11, 8, 11½)" (20.5 [28, 20.5, 28] cm), ending after a WS row.

NEXT ROW: (RS; dec row) K1, k2tog 0 (1, 0, 1) time(s), work in St st to last 1 (3, 1, 3) st(s), ssk 0 (1, 0, 1) time(s), k1—71 (79, 81, 89) sts rem.

Work even until piece measures 12¾ (12¾, 13, 13)" (32 [32, 33, 33] cm), ending after a WS row.

NEXT ROW: (RS; inc row) K1, k1f&b 1 (0, 1, 0) time(s), knit to last 1 (2, 1, 2) st(s), k1f&b 1 (0, 1, 0) time(s), k1—71 (81, 81, 91) sts.

Work even until piece measures 13¾ (13¾, 14¼, 14¼)" (35 [35, 36, 36] cm), ending after a WS row.

NEXT ROW: (RS; inc row) K1, k1f&b, knit to last 2 sts, k1f&b, k1—73 (83, 83, 93) sts.

Work even in St st until piece measures 15 (15½, 15¾, 16¼)" (38 [39, 40, 41] cm).

SHAPE ARMHOLES (BOTH JACKETS)

BO 2 (4, 3, 5) sts at beg of next 2 rows, 2 sts at beg of next 2 (4, 4, 6) rows, 1 st at beg of next 4 (4, 4, 4) rows—61 (63, 65, 67) sts rem.

Work even until armholes measure 7½ (7¾, 8¼, 8¾)" (19 [20, 21, 22] cm), ending after a WS row.

SHAPE NECK AND SHOULDERS (BOTH JACKETS)

NEXT ROW: (RS) K16 (17, 17, 18), join another ball of yarn and BO 29 (29, 31, 31) sts for neck, knit rem 16 (17, 17, 18) sts. Work each side separately and *at the same time* BO 8 (8, 8, 9) sts at beg of each shoulder edge once, then 8 (9, 9, 9) sts once.

RIGHT FRONT

SHORT JACKET

CO 30 (35, 35, 40) sts loosely.

ROW 1: (WS) K1 (edge st), work 26 (31, 31, 36) sts foll Short Jacket Chart B (page 33) as indicated for your size, work 2 sts in St st, k1 (edge st).

Continue as established, following Chart B with garter st edges as established. After Chart B is completed, continue in lace pattern following Chart B *only* over 10 lace pattern sts 3 sts in from front edge, working rem sts in St st. Work until piece measures 4" (10 cm) from CO, ending after a WS row.

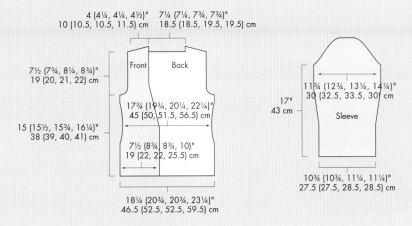

LONG JACKET

4 (4¼, 4¼, 4½)"
10 (10.5, 10.5, 11.5) cm

7¼ (7¼, 7¾, 7¾)"
18.5 (18.5, 19.5, 19.5) cm

7½ (7¾, 8¼, 8¾)"
19 (20, 21, 22) cm

Front   Back

17¾ (19¾, 20¼, 22¼)"
45 (50, 51.5, 56.5) cm

15 (15½, 15¾, 16¼)"
38 (39, 40, 41) cm

7½ (8¾, 8¾, 10)"
19 (22, 22, 25.5) cm

18¼ (20¾, 20¾, 23¼)"
46.5 (52.5, 52.5, 59.5) cm

11¾ (12¾, 13¼, 14¼)"
30 (32.5, 33.5, 30) cm

17"
43 cm

Sleeve

10¾ (10¾, 11¼, 11¼)"
27.5 (27.5, 28.5, 28.5) cm

LONG JACKET

With larger needles, CO 30 (35, 35, 40) sts loosely.

Row 1: (WS) K1 (edge st), work 26 (31, 31, 36) sts foll Short Jacket Chart B (page 33) as indicated for your size, work 2 sts in St st, k1 (edge st).

Continue as established, following Chart B with garter st edges as established. After Chart B is completed, continue in lace pattern following Chart B *only* over 10 lace pattern sts 3 sts from front edge and work rem sts in St st and *at the same time* shape waist as for back. Work until piece measures 10¼" (26 cm) from CO, ending after a WS row.

SHAPE NECK (BOTH JACKETS)

Next row: (RS) Cont as established and *at the same time* work 2 patt sts

tog at the front edge on this row, then every 1½" (4 cm) 6 (8, 7, 9) more times and *at the same time* shape waist as for back—23 (26, 27, 30) sts rem after all neck and waist shaping is complete. (*Note:* For long jacket, keep sts in patt as long as possible. After completing all decs, 1 patt st will rem for sizes S and M; this should be continued in St st as for rest of sts across.)

SHAPE ARMHOLE AND SHOULDER (BOTH JACKETS)

When at same length as back to armhole, BO at beg of armhole edge 3 (3, 4, 4) sts once, 2 sts 1 (2, 2, 3) time(s), 1 st 2 (2, 2, 2) times—16 (17, 17, 18) sts rem. Work even until armholes measure 7½ (8, 8¼, 8¾)" (19 [20, 21, 22] cm), ending after a RS row.

BO at beg of shoulder edge 8 (8, 8, 9) sts once, then 8 (9, 9, 9) sts once.

LEFT FRONT

SHORT JACKET

With size 8 needles, CO 30 (35, 35, 40) sts loosely.

Row 1: (WS) K1, work 2 sts in St st, work 26 (31, 31, 36) sts following Chart C, k1.

Cont as established, following Chart C Rows 2–8.

After charted pattern is completed, continue in lace pattern following Chart C *only* over 10 lace pattern sts at front edge working rem sts in St st. Work until piece measures 4" (10 cm), ending after a WS row.

LONG JACKET

CO 30 (35, 35, 40) sts loosely.

Row 1: (WS) K1, work 2 sts in St st, work 26 (31, 31, 36) sts following Chart C, k1.

Continue as established following Chart C Rows 2–8 with garter st edges as established.

CHART AI (LONG)

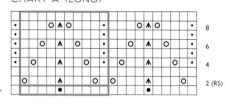

Bobble row (WS) →

CHART A (LONG)

Bobble row (WS) →

CHART A (SHORT)

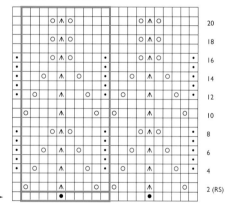

Bobble row (WS) →

☐ Knit

⊡ Purl

◺ Ssk

◿ K2tog

◉ Yarnover

⊼ Sl 2 as if to k2tog, k1, p2sso

⦿ Bobble: (P1, k1, p1) in the same st (3 sts), *turn, k1, p1, k1; rep from * two more times. Pass the 2nd and 3rd sts over the first st—1 st rem.

☐ Pattern repeat

CHART B (LONG)

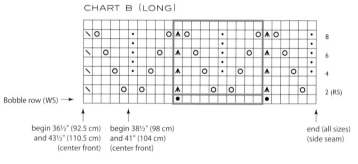

Bobble row (WS) →

begin 36½" (92.5 cm)
and 43½" (110.5 cm)
(center front)

begin 38½" (98 cm)
and 41" (104 cm)
(center front)

end (all sizes)
(side seam)

CHART B (SHORT)

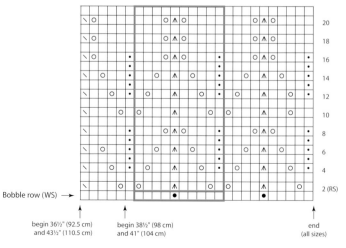

Bobble row (WS) →

begin 36½" (92.5 cm)
and 43½" (110.5 cm)

begin 38½" (98 cm)
and 41" (104 cm)

end
(all sizes)

After charted pattern is completed, cont in lace pattern following Chart C *only* over 10 lace pattern sts at front edge and working rem sts in St st and *at the same time* shape waist as for back. Work until piece measures 10¼" (26 cm) from CO, ending after a WS row.

SHAPE NECK (BOTH JACKETS)

NEXT ROW: (RS) Cont as established and *at the same time* shape waist as for back and *at the same time* work 2 patt sts tog at the front edge on this row, then every 1½" (4 cm) 6 (8, 7, 9) more times—23 (26, 27, 30) sts rem after all neck and waist shaping is complete. (*Note:* For long jacket, keep sts in patt as long as possible. After completing all decs, 1 patt st will rem for sizes S and M; this should be continued in St st as for rest of sts across.)

SHAPE ARMHOLE AND SHOULDER (BOTH JACKETS)

When at same length as back to armhole, shape armhole. BO at beg of armhole edge 3 (3, 4, 4) sts once, 2 sts 1 (2, 2, 3) time(s), and 1 st 2 times—16 (17, 17, 18) sts rem. Work even until armholes measure 7½ (8, 8¼, 8¾)" (19 [20, 21, 22] cm), ending after a WS row.

BO at beg of shoulder edge 8 (8, 8, 8, 9) sts once, then 8 (9, 9, 9) sts once.

SLEEVES

SHORT JACKET

With size 8 needles, CO 43 (45, 47, 47) sts.

ROW 1: (WS) K1, work 0 (1, 2, 2) st(s) in St st, work Chart A for 41 sts, work 0 (1, 2, 2) st(s) in St st, k1.

Continue in patt as established (foll Chart A, keeping extra sts in St st and working the first and last st in every row in garter st). After completing chart, rep Rows 17–20 two more times. Work even in St st until piece measures 5½" (14 cm), ending after a WS row.

NEXT ROW: (RS) K1, k1f&b 0 (1, 1, 1) time(s), knit to last 2 sts, k1f&b 0 (1, 1, 1) time(s), k1—43 (47, 49, 49) sts.

Work even in St st until piece measures 6 (6, 6, 6¼)" (15 [15, 15, 16] cm), ending after a WS row.

NEXT ROW: (RS) K1, k1f&b 1 (0, 0, 1) time(s), knit to last 2 (1, 2, 1) st(s), k1f&b 1 (0, 0, 1) time(s), k1—45 (47, 49, 51) sts.

Work even in St st until piece measures 7 (7, 7, 7½)" (18 [18, 18, 19] cm), ending after a WS row.

NEXT ROW: (RS) K1, k1f&b 0 (1, 1, 1) time(s), knit to last 1 (2, 2, 2) st(s), k1f&b 0 (1, 1, 1) time(s), k1—45 (49, 51, 53) sts.

Work even in St st until piece measures 8 (8¾, 8¾, 8¼)" (20.5 [22, 22, 21] cm), ending after a WS row.

NEXT ROW: (RS) K1, k1f&b, knit to last 2 sts, k1f&b, k1—47 (51, 53, 55) sts.

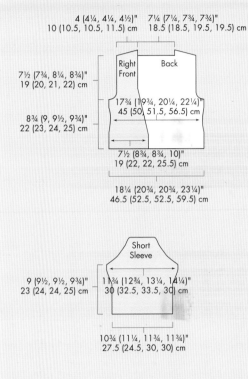

SHORT JACKET

4 (4¼, 4¼, 4½)"
10 (10.5, 10.5, 11.5) cm

7¼ (7¼, 7¾, 7¾)"
18.5 (18.5, 19.5, 19.5) cm

7½ (7¾, 8¼, 8¾)"
19 (20, 21, 22) cm

Right Front   Back

17¾ (19¾, 20¼, 22¼)"
45 (50, 51.5, 56.5) cm

8¾ (9, 9½, 9¾)"
22 (23, 24, 25) cm

7½ (8¾, 8¾, 10)"
19 (22, 22, 25.5) cm

18¼ (20¾, 20¾, 23¼)"
46.5 (52.5, 52.5, 59.5) cm

Short Sleeve

9 (9½, 9½, 9¾)"
23 (24, 24, 25) cm

11¾ (12¾, 13¼, 14¼)"
30 (32.5, 33.5, 30) cm

10¾ (11¼, 11¾, 11¾)"
27.5 (24.5, 30, 30) cm

LARGEST SIZE ONLY

Work even in St st until piece measures 9" (23 cm), ending after a WS row.

NEXT ROW: (RS) K1, k1f&b, knit to last 2 sts, k1f&b, k1—57 sts.

ALL SIZES

Work even in St st until piece measures 9 (9½, 9½, 9¾)" (23 [24, 24, 25] cm).

LONG JACKET

With size 10 needles, CO 43 (43, 45, 45) sts.

ROW 1: (WS) K1, work 0 (0, 1, 1) st(s) in St st, work chart A for 41 sts, work 0 (0, 1, 1) st(s) in St st, k1.

Continue in patt as established (foll Chart A, keeping extra sts in St st, and working the first and last st in every row in garter st). After completing chart, work even in St st until piece measures 6¼ (6, 6, 6)" (16 [15, 15, 15] cm), ending after a WS row.

NEXT ROW: (RS) K1, k1f&b, work in St st to last 2 sts, k1f&b, k1—45 (45, 47, 47) sts.

Work even in patt until piece measures 8¾ (8¾, 8¾, 8)" (22 [22, 22, 20.5] 5 cm), ending after a WS row.

NEXT ROW: (RS) K1, k1f&b 0 (1, 1, 1) time(s), work in St st to last 2 sts, k1f&b 0 (1, 1, 1) time(s), k1—45 (47, 49, 49) sts.

LARGEST SIZE ONLY

Work even in patt until piece measures 9¾" (35 cm), ending after a WS row.

NEXT ROW: (RS) K1, k1f&b, work in St st to last 2 sts, k1f&b, k1—51 sts.

ALL SIZES

Work even in patt until piece measures 11½ (11½, 11½, 11¾)" (29 [29, 29, 30] cm), ending after a WS row.

NEXT ROW: (RS) K1, k1f&b 0 (1, 1, 1) time(s), work in St st to last 1 (2, 2, 2) st(s), k1f&b 0 (1, 1, 1) time(s), k1—45 (49, 51, 53) sts.

Work even in patt until piece measures 12¾ (12¾, 12¾, 13¼)" (32.5 [32.5, 32.5, 33.5] cm), ending after a WS row.

NEXT ROW: (RS) K1, k1f&b 1 (0, 0, 1) time(s), work in St st to last st, k1f&b 1 (0, 0, 1) time(s), k1—47 (49, 51, 55) sts.

Work even in patt until piece measures 14¼ (14¼, 14¼, 15¾)" (36 [36, 36, 40] cm), ending after a WS row.

NEXT ROW: (RS) K1, k1f&b 0 (1, 1, 1) time(s), work in St st to last 1 (2, 2, 2) st(s), k1f&b 0 (1, 1, 1) time(s), k1—47 (51, 53, 57) sts.

Work even in patt until piece measures 17" (43 cm) from CO or desired length.

CHART C (LONG)

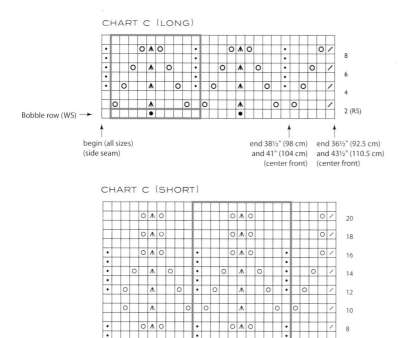

Bobble row (WS) →

begin (all sizes)
(side seam)

end 38½" (98 cm)
and 41" (104 cm)
(center front)

end 36½" (92.5 cm)
and 43½" (110.5 cm)
(center front)

8
6
4
2 (RS)

CHART C (SHORT)

Bobble row (WS) →

begin
(all sizes)
(side seam)

end 38½" (98 cm)
and 41" (104 cm)
(center front)

end 36½" (92.5 cm)
and 43½" (110.5 cm)
(center front)

20
18
16
14
12
10
8
6
4
2 (RS)

☐ Knit

• Purl

◺ Ssk

◿ K2tog

◯ Yarnover

⟁ Sl 2 as if to k2tog, k1, p2sso

● Bobble: (P1, k1, p1) in the same st (3 sts), *turn, k1, p1, k1; rep from * two more times. Pass the 2nd and 3rd sts over the first st—1 st rem.

☐ Pattern repeat

33

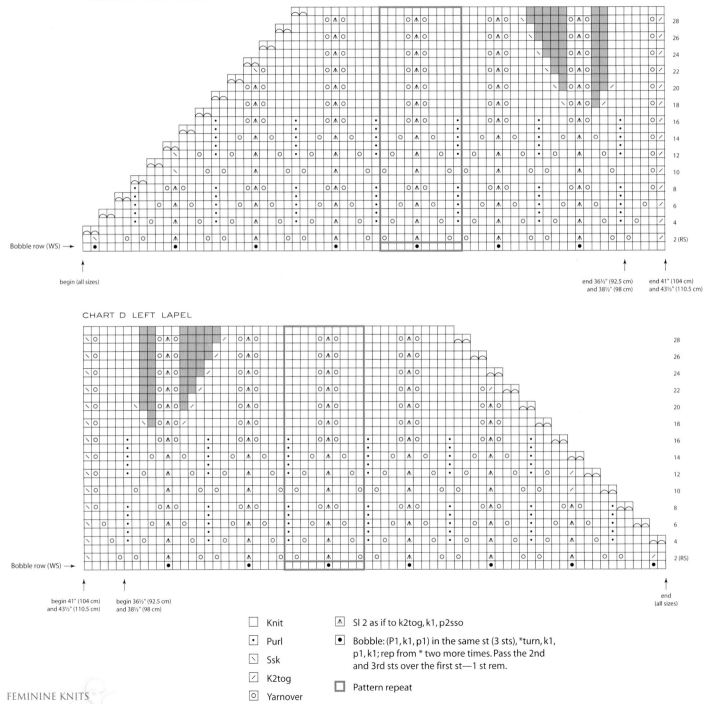

CHART D RIGHT LAPEL

Bobble row (WS) →

begin (all sizes)

end 36½" (92.5 cm)
and 38½" (98 cm)

end 41" (104 cm)
and 43½" (110.5 cm)

CHART D LEFT LAPEL

Bobble row (WS) →

begin 41" (104 cm)
and 43½" (110.5 cm)

begin 36½" (92.5 cm)
and 38½" (98 cm)

end
(all sizes)

	Knit		⋀	Sl 2 as if to k2tog, k1, p2sso
	Purl		●	Bobble: (P1, k1, p1) in the same st (3 sts), *turn, k1, p1, k1; rep from * two more times. Pass the 2nd and 3rd sts over the first st—1 st rem.
	Ssk			
	K2tog			Pattern repeat
	Yarnover			

SHAPE CAP (BOTH JACKETS)

BO 3 (3, 4, 4) sts at beg of next 2 rows, 2 sts at beg of next 4 rows, 1 st at beg of next 14 (14, 10, 10) rows. BO 2 (2, 2, 3) sts at beg of next 2 rows, 2 (2, 3, 4) sts at beg of next 2 rows, then 3 (4, 4, 4) sts at beg of next 2 rows. BO rem 5 (7, 9, 9) sts.

FINISHING

With yarn threaded on a tapestry needle, use invisible horizontal method (see Glossary) to sew shoulder seams.

RIGHT LAPEL

With smaller needles, CO 99 (99, 104, 104) sts for right half of collar. Beg with a WS row and working first and last sts of every row in garter st (not shown on chart), work Chart D, binding off sts at beg of WS rows as indicated. BO all sts.

LEFT LAPEL

With smaller needles, CO 99 (99, 104, 104) sts for left half of collar. Beg with a WS row and working first and last sts of every row in garter st (not shown on chart), work Chart D, binding off sts at beg of RS rows as indicated. BO all sts.

BOTH LAPELS

Pin each lapel in place with WS of lapel facing RS of front. With yarn threaded on a tapestry needle, sew in place using a backstitch. For long jacket, the collar begins about 6¼" (16 cm) from lower edge; ease any extra length on the collar into rounded edge of the collar and at shoulders. For short jacket, lapel begins at lower front edge. Using a backstitch, seam two short ends of collar where they meet at center back.

Sew shoulder, underarm, and side seams.

LONG JACKET ONLY

*With smaller needles, pick up and knit about 26 (30, 32, 36) sts along front edge from 6¼" (16 cm) from lower left front to beginning of collar. Knit 1 row. BO knitwise. Rep from * for right front edge.

SHORT AND LONG JACKETS
CORD

With crochet hook and yarn held double, make a crochet chain (see Glossary) about 50" (127 cm) long; fasten off. Thread cord through body of sweater at waist between every 4th and 5th st.

BOBBLES

With crochet hook, crochet 2 bobbles as foll: Ch 6, 6 dbl tr into first ch but do not pull last yarn over through for each st (7 sts loops on hook when all 6 dbl tr have been worked). Yarn over hook and pull through all 7 loops. Sew 1 bobble securely to each end of cord.

bolero

This light little piece looks lovely over a summer dress, perfect to cover your shoulders. The linen in the yarn gives the stitches good definition, showing off the lace pattern and preventing the jacket from stretching. It also keeps the jacket lightweight and breathable.

FINISHED MEASUREMENTS
33½ (36¼, 38½, 41)" (85 [92, 98, 104] cm) bust circumference, 17¾ (18½, 19¼, 20)" (45 [47, 49, 51] cm) length from CO to neck edge.

YARN
Fingering weight (Super Fine #1).
Shown here: Coats HP Løve Lima (38% linen, 31% cotton; 31% viscose; 223 yd [104 m]/50 g): #211 powder, 2 (3, 3, 3) balls. See page 126 for yarn substitution suggestions.

NEEDLES
U.S. size 1.5 (2.5 mm) and U.S. size 4 (3.5 mm): straight. U.S. size 1.5 (2.5 mm): 24" (60 cm) circular (cir). Adjust needle sizes if necessary to obtain the correct gauge.

NOTIONS
Large-eye tapestry needle; stitch holders; about 67" (170 cm) of ¾" wide ribbon.

GAUGE
19 sts and 36 rows = 4" (10 cm) in lace pattern on larger needles.

NOTE
Work the first and last stitch of every row in garter stitch (knit on RS and WS).

stitch guide

LACE PATTERN

(multiple of 6 sts plus 5,
  including garter st edges)

Row 1: (RS) K4, *yo, sl 1,
  k2tog, psso, yo, k3; rep
  from * to last st, k1.

Row 2: K1, purl to last st, k1.

Row 3: K1, yo, sl 1, k2tog,
  psso, yo, *k3, yo, sl 1, k2tog,
  psso, yo; rep from * to last
  st, k1.

Row 4: Rep Row 2.

Repeat Rows 1–4 for patt.

RIBBING PATTERN

(multiple of 6 sts plus 2 garter
  st edges)

Row 1: (WS) K1, *k3, p3; rep
  from * to last st, k1.

Row 2: K1, *k3, p3; rep from
  * to last st, k1.

Rep Rows 1–2 for patt.

NOTES

· Work increased and
  decreased stitches into Lace
  pattern. If there are not
  enough stitches available to
  complete a double decrease
  (sl 1, k2tog, psso), work
  k2tog at beginning of row
  and ssk at end of row.

· If there are not enough
  stitches available to work
  a complete Lace pattern
  repeat, end 3 stitches before
  end of pattern repeat and
  work rem sts in St st.

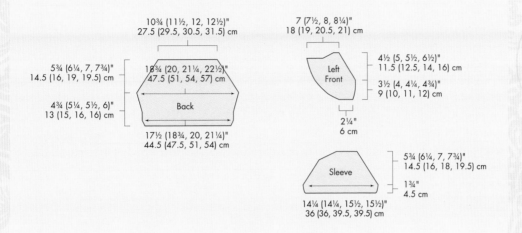

10¾ (11½, 12, 12½)"
27.5 (29.5, 30.5, 31.5) cm

7 (7½, 8, 8¼)"
18 (19, 20.5, 21) cm

5¾ (6¼, 7, 7¾)"
14.5 (16, 19, 19.5) cm

18¾ (20, 21¼, 22½)"
47.5 (51, 54, 57) cm

4½ (5, 5½, 6½)"
11.5 (12.5, 14, 16) cm

Left Front

3½ (4, 4¼, 4¾)"
9 (10, 11, 12) cm

4¾ (5¼, 5½, 6)"
13 (15, 16, 16) cm

Back

2¼"
6 cm

17½ (18¾, 20, 21¼)"
44.5 (47.5, 51, 54) cm

5¾ (6¼, 7, 7¾)"
14.5 (16, 18, 19.5) cm

Sleeve

1¾"
4.5 cm

14¼ (14¼, 15½, 15½)"
36 (36, 39.5, 39.5) cm

BACK

With smaller straight needles, CO 104 (110, 116, 122) sts. Beg with a WS row, work Ribbing patt for 1¼" (3 cm), ending after a RS row. With larger needles, k1, purl to last st and *at the same time* dec 21 sts evenly across row to last st, k1—83 (89, 95, 101) sts rem.

Work Lace patt (see Stitch Guide) until piece measures 1½ (2, 2, 1½)" (4 [5, 5, 4] cm) from beg of Lace patt, ending after a WS row. NEXT ROW: (RS; inc row) K1, k1f&b, work in patt to last st, k1f&b, k1—85 (91, 97, 103) sts. Work in patt until piece measures 2½ (2¾, 2¾, 2¾)" (6.5 [7, 7, 7] cm) from beg of Lace patt, ending after a WS row. Rep inc row—87 (93, 99, 105) sts.

Work in patt until piece measures 3¼ (3½, 3½, 4)" (8.5 [9, 9, 10] cm) from beg of Lace patt, end-

ing after a WS row. Rep inc row—89 (95, 101, 107) sts.

Work even in patt until piece measures 3½ (4, 4¼, 4¾)" (9 [10, 11, 12] cm) from end of ribbing, ending after Row 4 of Lace patt.

RAGLAN SHAPING
(RS; dec row) K2, ssk, work in patt to last 4 sts, k2tog, k2—2 sts dec'd.

Rep dec row alternately every 4th and 2nd row until a total of 18 (19, 21, 23) dec rows have been worked—53 (57, 59, 61) sts rem. BO 1 st at beg of next 2 rows—51 (55, 57, 59) sts rem. Place sts on a holder.

LEFT FRONT

Note: Read the following directions before working further, as several actions as performed at the same time.

With larger needles, CO 11 sts. Purl 1 row. Work Lace patt, increas-

ing 1 st as k1f&b at side seam when piece measures 1½ (2, 2, 1½)" (4 [5, 5, 4] cm) from CO, then at 2½ (2¾, 2¾, 2¾)" (6.5 [7, 7, 7] cm) from CO, then at 3¼ (3½, 3½, 4)" (8.5 [9, 9, 10] cm) from CO and *at the same time* CO new sts at the end of RS rows for rounded edge as foll: 3 sts 2 (2, 3, 3) times, 2 sts 2 (3, 2, 3) times, then k1f&b at front edge every other row 12 (13, 15, 16) times, then every 4th row 7 (8, 9, 9) times, working new sts into patt and *at the same time* when piece measures 3½ (4, 4¼, 4¾)" (9 [10, 11, 12] cm) from CO, ending after Row 4 of Lace patt, shape raglan on side edge as k2tog two sts from side edge on next RS row, then every 4th and 2nd rows alternately, until 10 (11, 13, 15) raglan dec rows have been worked—33 (36, 38, 39) sts rem.

On next WS row, place first 12 (13, 14, 15) sts at front edge on holder—21 (23, 24, 24) sts on ndl. Continue raglan shaping (k2tog two sts from side edge) alternating every 4th and 2nd rows until 4 more dec rows have been worked and *at the same time* BO 4 sts at beg of next 3 WS rows at neck edge. BO 5 (7, 8, 8) rem sts. *Note:* Front pieces are about 3 raglan decs (18 rows) shorter than back.

RIGHT FRONT

With larger needles, CO 11 sts. Purl 1 row. Work Lace patt and inc 1 st as k1f&b at side seam when piece measures 1½ (2, 2, 1½)" (4 [5, 5, 4] cm) from CO, then at 2½ (2¾, 2¾, 2¾)" (6.5 [7, 7, 7] cm) from CO, then at 3¼ (3½, 3½, 4)" (8.5 [9, 9, 10] cm) from CO and *at the same time* CO new sts at the end of RS rows for rounded edge as foll: 3 sts 2 (2, 3, 3) times, 2 sts 2 (3, 2, 3) times, then k1f&b at front edge every other row 12 (13, 15, 16) times, then every 4th row 7 (8, 9, 9) times, working new sts into patt and *at the same time* when piece measures 3½ (4, 4¼, 4¾)" (9 [10, 11, 12] cm) from CO, ending after Row 4 of Lace patt, shape raglan on side edge as ssk two sts from side edge on next RS row, then every 4th and 2nd rows alternately until 10 (11, 13, 15) raglan dec rows have been worked—33 (36, 38, 39) sts rem. On next RS row, place first 12 (13, 14, 15) sts at front

edge on holder. Continue raglan shaping as ssk two sts from side edge on next RS row, then every 4th and 2nd rows until 4 more dec rows have been worked and *at the same time* BO 4 sts at beg of next 3 RS rows at neck edge. BO 5 (7, 8, 8) rem sts. *Note:* Front pieces are about 3 raglan decs (18 rows) shorter than back.

RIGHT SLEEVE

With smaller needles, CO 80 (80, 86, 86) sts. Work Ribbing pattern for 1¼" (3 cm), ending after a RS row. Change to larger needles, k1, purl to last st and *at the same time* dec 12 sts evenly across row as p2tog, k1—68 (68, 74, 74) sts rem.

Work Lace patt for 4 rows.

RAGLAN SHAPING

(RS) K2, k2tog, work in patt to last 4 sts rem, ssk, k2—2 sts dec'd.

Rep this dec row alternately every 4th and 2nd row until a total of 14 (15, 17, 19) dec rows have been worked—40 (38, 40, 36) sts rem. Continue raglan shaping as ssk two sts from back edge and *at the same time* *BO 3 sts at beg of next RS row, BO 4 sts at beg of next RS row; rep from * until 18 (19, 21, 23) raglan decs have been worked. BO rem sts.

LEFT SLEEVE

With smaller needles, CO 80 (80, 86, 86) sts. Work Ribbing pattern for 1¼" (3 cm), ending after a RS row. Change to larger needles, k1, purl to last st and *at the same time* dec 12 sts evenly across row as p2tog, k1—68 (68, 74, 74) sts rem.

Work Lace patt for 4 rows.

RAGLAN SHAPING

(RS) K2, k2tog, work in patt to last 4 sts rem, ssk, k2—2 sts dec'd.

Rep this dec row alternately every 4th and 2nd row until a total of 14 (15, 17, 19) dec rows have been worked and *at the same time* *BO 3 sts at beg of next RS row, BO 4 sts at beg of next RS row; rep from * until 18 (19, 21, 23) raglan decs have been worked. BO rem sts.

FINISHING

With cir needle, pick up and knit (see Glossary) 98 (104, 110, 116) sts along left front center and lower edge for left front ribbing. (*Note:* Pick up about 5 sts for every 4 pattern sts at lower edge and about 1 st for every row along front edge. Make sure the stitch count is a multiple of 6 + 2 edge sts.)

Next row: (WS) K1, *p3, k3; rep from * to last st, k1 (matching ribbing on back at side seam). Cont in Ribbing patt for 1¼" (3 cm). BO in patt.

With cir needle, pick up and knit 98 (104, 110, 116) sts along right front lower and center edge for right front ribbing. Work Ribbing patt as for left front ribbing for 1¼" (3 cm). BO in patt.

With yarn threaded on a tapestry needle, use invisible vertical method (see Glossary) to sew raglan, underarm, and side seams.

Place 12 (13, 14, 15) held sts from left front on cir needle, pick up and knit 81 (84, 88, 92) sts across right front and right sleeve, place 51 (55, 57, 59) held back sts on needle, pick up and knit 81 (84, 88, 92) sts along left sleeve and left front, place 12 (13, 14, 15) held sts from left front on needle—237 (249, 261, 273) sts total.

Next row: (WS) P3, *k3, p3; rep from * to end.

Next row: K3, *p3, k3; rep from * to end.

Rep last 2 rows until ribbing measures 1¼" (3 cm). BO all sts in patt.

Thread ribbon through tapestry needle. Lace ribbon through the center of the neckband, going in and out between center sts in each knit rib.

SHAWL WITH
leaf lace

The lace edging for this shawl is quite lovely and finely detailed. To keep the focus on the lace, the rest of the shawl is plain stockinette. Knitting the corners of the lace may be challenging, but the rest is smooth sailing.

FINISHED SIZE
63" (160 cm) wide across top edge.

YARN
Fingering weight (Super Fine #1).
Shown here: Coats HP Løve Lima (38% linen, 31% cotton; 31% viscose; 223 yd [104 m]/50 g): #02 white, 4 balls. See page 126 for yarn substitution suggestions.

NEEDLES
U.S. size 2 (3 mm): 32" (80 cm) circular (cir). Adjust needle size if necessary to obtain the correct gauge.

NOTIONS
Stitch markers (m), tapestry needle.

GAUGE
27 sts and 40 rows = 4" (10 cm) in stockinette stitch.

CORNER LEAF

Chart row numbers (right side, bottom to top): 1, 3, 5, 7, 9, 11, 13, 15, 17, 19, 21, 23, 25, 27, 29, 31, 33, 35 (corner), 37, 39, 41, 43, 45, 47, 49, 51, 53, 55, 57, 59, 61, 63, 65, 67

Legend

☐	Knit on RS; purl on WS
•	Purl on RS; knit on WS
○	Yarnover
╱	K2tog
╲	Ssk
↗	P2tog
V	Sl 1 wyb on RS; sl 1 wyf on WS
⋀	Sl 2 as if to k2tog; k1, p2sso
⌒	Bind off 1 st
(gray)	No stitch
☐	Pattern repeat

SHAWL

LACE BORDER

CO 15 sts. Purl 1 row. Work Rows 1–20 of Small Leaf chart 16 times. Work Corner Leaf chart and *at the same time* work short-rows as foll:

ROWS 1–7: Work Corner Leaf chart.

ROWS 8–9: Work chart Row 8 (WS) to last st, turn (leaving 1 unworked st held), work chart Row 9 (RS). (Tighten working yarn when turning.)

ROWS 10–11: Work chart Row 10 (WS) to last 2 sts (leaving 2 unworked sts held), turn, work chart Row 11 (RS).

Continue in this manner, leaving 1 additional unworked st held after every RS row, through chart Row 35—4 sts.

NEXT ROW: BO 3 sts, knit rem 2 sts and 1 unworked held st following chart.

Cont to follow chart, working 1 more held st every other row until all 15 sts are again being worked.

Work Small Leaf chart 16 more times. BO all sts.

STOCKINETTE PANELS

With RS facing, pick up and knit (see Glossary) 220 sts along right edge of leaf lace to turning st (about 13 sts in each leaf), pm, pick up and knit 1 st in corner, pick up and knit 220 sts along right edge to BO—441 sts. Knit 1 row on WS.

ROW 1: (RS) K2, k2tog, work to 2 sts before m, ssk, k1, k2tog, work to last 4 sts, ssk, k2—4 sts dec'd.

ROW 2: (WS) K2, purl to last 2 sts, k2.

ROWS 3–6: Rep Rows 1–2.

ROW 7: K2, k3tog, knit to 2 sts before m, ssk, k1, k2tog, knit to last 5 sts, sssk, k2—6 sts dec'd.

ROW 8: Rep Row 2.

Rep Rows 1–8 until 5 sts rem.

NEXT ROW: (RS) Sl 2, k3tog, p2sso—1 st rem. Cut yarn and pull tail through rem st. Weave in ends.

FINISHING

Dampen shawl and block firmly in triangle shape until dry, making sure that top edge is smooth and even.

SMALL LEAF

jacquard JACKET

The stranded pattern for this jacket creates a tightly knit fabric, which helps hold the jacket's shape. The classic silhouette is embellished with crochet details and embroidery for a less formal look.

FINISHED MEASUREMENTS

37 (41)" (94 [104] cm) bust circumference; 45¾ (49¾)" (116 [126] cm) wide at lower edge; 35½ (37)" (90 [94] cm) long.

YARN

Fingering weight (Super Fine #1).

Shown here: Sandnesgarn Sisu (80% wool, 20% nylon; 173 yd [158 m]/50 g): #1012 natural white, 9 (11) balls, #1042 gray, 6 (6) balls; #9544 green, 2 balls. See page 126 for yarn substitution suggestions.

NEEDLES

U.S. size 4 (3.5 mm): 16" and 32" (40 and 80 cm) circular (cir), set of 5 double-pointed (dpn). U.S. size D (3 mm) crochet hook. Adjust needle sizes if necessary to obtain the correct gauge.

NOTIONS

Tapestry needle; stitch markers (m); sewing machine and matching thread; eight ¾" (2 cm) buttons.

GAUGE

27 sts and 29 rows/rounds = 4" (10 cm) in stockinette stranded two-color knitting.

BODY

Note: Body is worked in the rnd to armholes with 4 center front steek sts to be cut open after knitting is complete.

With longer cir and natural, CO 312 (340) sts. Join for working in the rnd, being careful not to twist sts. Add gray yarn.

Set up patts: Work 2 sts following Steek chart, work 77 (84) sts following Jacquard chart for front, place marker (pm) for side seam, work 154 (168) sts following Jacquard chart for back, pm for side seam, work 77 (84) sts following Jacquard chart for front, work 2 sts following Steek chart. Rnd begins at center of 4 steek sts.

Cont in patt as established, following Jacquard chart for fronts and back and Steek chart for 4 center sts, until jacket measures 7 (7½)" (18 [19] cm) from CO.

NEXT RND: (dec rnd) *Work in patt to 2 sts before m, ssk, k2tog; rep from * once more, work in patt to end of rnd—4 sts dec'd.

Rep dec round every 5th round 17 more times—240 (268) sts rem after last dec. Cont in patt until jacket measures 20½ (21¼)" (52 [54] cm) from CO.

NEXT ROW: (inc rnd) Working incs into Jacquard patt, *work in patt to 1 st before m, M1 (see Glossary), k2, M1; rep from * once more, work in patt to end of rnd—4 sts inc'd.

Rep inc rnd every 1½" (4 cm) 3 more times—256 (284) sts. Work until jacket measures 26½ (27¼)" (67 [69] cm).

NEXT RND: K2tog (2 steek sts), work 63 (70) sts following Jacquard chart and place 64 (71) sts just worked on a holder for left front, work 126 (140) sts following Jacquard chart for back; work 63 (70) sts following Jacquard chart, k2tog (2 steek sts), place 64 (71) sts just worked on a holder for right front, remove second m.

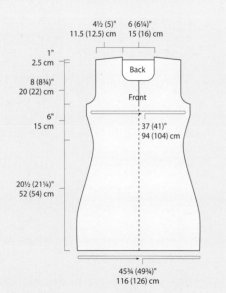

4½ (5)"
11.5 (12.5) cm

6 (6¼)"
15 (16) cm

1"
2.5 cm

Back

8 (8¾)"
20 (22) cm

Front

6"
15 cm

37 (41)"
94 (104) cm

20½ (21¼)"
52 (54) cm

45¾ (49¾)"
116 (126) cm

Sleeve

14¼ (15¾)"
36 (40) cm

16½"
42 cm

9¾ (10½)"
25 (26.5) cm

BACK

SHAPE ARMHOLE

Reattach yarn to back sts and begin working back and forth in rows.

BO 3 (4) sts at beg of next 2 rows, 2 (3) sts at beg of next 2 rows, 2 sts at beg of next 2 rows, 1 (2) sts at beg of next 2 rows, 1 st at beg of next 8 rows—102 (110) sts rem. Work even in patt until armhole measures 8 (8¾)" (20 [22] cm), ending after a WS row.

SHAPE NECK AND SHOULDERS

NEXT ROW: (RS) K31 (34), join another ball of yarn and BO center 40 (42) sts for neck, k31 (34). Working each side separately, BO 10 (11) sts at armhole edge 2 times, then BO 11 (12) sts at armhole edge once.

RIGHT FRONT

SHAPE ARMHOLE

Place right front sts from holder onto needles. BO at beg of armhole edge every other row 3 (4) sts once, 2 (3) sts once, 2 sts once, 1 (2) st(s) once, then 1 st 4 times—54 (58) sts rem. Work even in patt until armhole measures 4¼ (5¼)" (11 [13] cm), ending after a WS row.

SHAPE NECK AND SHOULDER

BO at beg of neck edge every other row 13 (14) sts once, 3 sts once, 2 sts twice, 1 st 3 times—31 (34) sts rem.

Work until armhole measures same length as back. BO 10 (11) sts at beg of next 2 WS rows, then BO 11 (12) sts at beg of next WS row.

LEFT FRONT

SHAPE ARMHOLE

Place left front sts from holder onto needles. BO at beg of armhole edge every other row 3 (4) sts once, 2 (3) sts once, 2 sts once, 1 (2) st(s) once, then 1 st 4 times—54 (58) sts rem. Work even in patt until armhole measures 4¼ (5¼)" (11 [13] cm), ending after a WS row.

SHAPE NECK AND SHOULDER

BO at beg of neck edge every other row 13 (14) sts once, 3 sts once, 2 sts twice, 1 st 3 times—31 (34) sts rem. Work until armhole measures same length as back. BO 10 (11) sts at beg of next 2 RS rows, then BO 11 (12) sts at beg of next RS row.

SLEEVES

With dpn and natural, CO 65 (71) sts. Join for working in the round, being careful not to twist sts, and knit 1 round. Work Jacquard chart as indicated for size to last st, p1 (underarm st). Work in patt until sleeve measures 3¼ (2½)" (8 [6] cm).

NEXT RND: (inc rnd) Work in patt to last st, M1, p1, M1—2 sts inc'd.

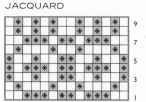

JACQUARD

9
7
5
3
1

STEEK

1

↑
center front

☐ With white, knit on RS; purl on WS

◈ With gray, knit on RS; purl on WS

☐ Pattern repeat

Rep inc row every ¾" (2 cm) 15 (17) more times, working new sts into patt—97 (107) sts. Change to shorter cir when desired. When sleeve measures 16½" (42 cm) or desired length, BO underarm st; begin to work back and forth in rows.

SHAPE SLEEVE CAP

BO 3 sts at beg of next 2 (4) rows, then 2 sts at beg of next 8 rows, 1 st at beg of next 22 (24) rows. BO 2 sts at beg of next 12 rows, then 3 sts at beg of next 4 rows. BO rem 17 (19) sts.

FINISHING

Machine-stitch two rows of small straight sts on each side of 4 steek sts at center front. Cut open between stitch lines at center front and then zigzag over the cut edges.

CROCHET EDGING

With green, crochet 1 round of sc along sleeve edge as foll: *Sc in each of next 5 sts, skip next st; rep from * to end, sl st to first sc to join (see Glossary for crochet directions). Turn and sc 1 row. Continue working back and forth in sc, joining each row with 1 sl st before you turn so you won't have to sew the edging together. When sc edging measures 1¼" (3 cm), finish with a row of shrimp st crochet from RS.

With green, work in sc down left front band, along lower edge, and up right front band and *at the same time* at the lower front corners work 3 sc into same st on every row to create a corner. When the bands are ⅝" (1.5 cm) wide, make 6 buttonholes, with the top one at top of front band and the lowest about 9¾" (25 cm) from lower edge and the other 4 spaced evenly between. *Buttonhole:* Skip 4 sc and ch 4 over gap. Work until edging measures 1¼" (3 cm). Sew shoulder seams. Sew buttons opposite buttonholes.

With green, crochet a row of about 116 (120) sc on RS along neck edge (begin and end at center of band). Turn. Continue in sc and inc 1 sc at each shoulder on every 4th row a total of 4 times; then inc 1 sc at each side of every 4th row until collar measures 3½" (9 cm). Continue in sc and sc2tog at each side of the next 4 rows. Fasten off.

With green, work 1 row of sc around collar and the top ends of front bands on what will be RS of collar. Finish with 1 row of shrimp st along the edges of collar, bands, and lower edge. Sew in sleeves.

For button panel on jacket back, ch 30 with green. Sc in 2nd loop from hook, work 1 sc in each ch across row, ending with 2 sc in next to last ch, 1 sc in last ch. Do not turn, but continue working around other side of chain, working 1 sc in first ch, 2 sc in next ch, then 1 sc in each ch across, ending with 1 sl st in the first sc to join. Continue working around in sc for a total of 5 rounds and *at the same time* crochet 2 sc in each corner st so that the corners will be rounded (there will be 2 sts more between incs at the ends for each rnd). End with 1 rnd

shrimp st. Sew button panel to back centered at waist height. Sew two buttons on button panel.

EMBROIDERY

Use daisy and French knot sts to embroider flowers and leaves at lower edge of left front as shown. (See Glossary for embroidery instructions.)

lace circle
SWEATER

This intricate lace jacket is a bit challenging to knit but uses only three balls of yarn for the smaller size. You are guaranteed many hours of enjoyable knitting, and you'll finish with a lovely and unique jacket.

FINISHED MEASUREMENTS
About 19¾ (21¾)" (50 [55] cm) width from armhole to armhole; about 26½ (27½)" (67 [70] cm) back length. (Jacket is very elastic, so only two sizes are given.)

YARN
DK weight (#3 Light).
Shown here: Coats Fonty Kidopale (70% kid mohair, 30% polyamide; 275 yd [250 m]/25 g): #308 blue, 3 (4) balls. See page 126 for yarn substitution suggestions.

NEEDLES
U.S. size 9 (5.5 mm) for smaller size; U.S. size 10 (6 mm) for larger size: set of 5 double-pointed (dpn), 16" (40) and 24" or 32" (60 or 80 cm) circular (cir). Adjust needle size if necessary to obtain the correct gauge.

NOTIONS
Stitch markers (m) in at least 2 colors; tapestry needle.

GAUGE
16 sts = 4" (10 cm) in stockinette stitch with smaller needle. 14 sts = 4" (10 cm) in stockinette stitch with larger needle.

BACK

Note: Sizes are determined by needle size.

With dpns as indicated for your size, CO 8 sts and arrange evenly on 4 dpns. Join for working in the rnd, being careful not to twist sts.

Note: Change to cir needles when there are too many sts to work comfortably on dpns; pm on cir to correspond with end of each dpn. Mark beg of rnd with different color m.

RNDS I AND 2: Knit.

RND 3: [Yo, k1] 8 times—16 sts.

RNDS 4–6: Knit.

RND 7: [Yo, k1] 16 times—32 sts.

RNDS 8–12: Knit.

Note: On the following rnds, work from * 2 times on each needle, 8 times total to end of rnd.

RND 13: *K2tog, 2 yo, ssk; rep from * to end of rnd—32 sts.

RND 14: *K1, slip next yo off left needle, knit into the [front, back, front, back, front, back, front, back, front] of next yo (9 sts total), k1 (22 sts on each ndl); rep from * to end of rnd—88 sts.

RNDS 15–24: Knit.

RND 25: *Yo, k11; rep from * to end of rnd—96 sts.

RND 26 AND ALL EVEN-NUMBERED ROUNDS TO RND 52: Knit.

RND 27: *Yo, k1, yo, k11; rep from * to end of rnd—112 sts.

RND 29: *Yo, k3, yo, k4, sl 1, k2tog, psso, k4; rep from * to end of rnd—112 sts.

RND 31: *Yo, k1, yo, 1 sl 1, k2tog, psso, yo, k1, yo, k3, sl 1, k2tog, psso, k3; rep from * to end of rnd—112 sts.

RND 33: *Yo, k3, yo, k1f&b, yo, k3, yo, k2, sl 1, k2tog, psso, k2; rep from * to end of rnd—136 sts.

RND 35: *Yo, k1, yo, sl 1, k2tog, psso, yo, k4, yo, sl 1, k2tog, psso, [yo, k1] 2 times, sl 1, k2tog, psso, k1; rep from * to end of rnd—136 sts.

RND 37: *Yo, k3, yo, k2, ssk, k2tog, k2, yo, k3, yo, sl 1, k2tog, psso; rep from * to end of rnd—136 sts.

RND 39: *Yo, k1, yo, sl 1, k2tog, psso, yo, k2, ssk, k2tog, k2, yo, sl 1, k2tog, psso, [yo, k1] 2 times; rep from * to end of rnd—136 sts.

RND 41: *[Yo, k3] 2 times, ssk, k2tog, [k3, yo] 2 times, k1; rep from * to end of rnd—152 sts.

RND 43: *Yo, k1, yo, sl 1, k2tog, psso, yo, k3, ssk, k2tog, k3, yo, sl 1, k2tog, psso, [yo, k1] 2 times; rep from * to end—152 sts.

RND 45: Knit.

RND 47: *[Yo, k1] 2 times, yo, k3, ssk 2 times, k2tog 2 times, k3 [yo, k1] 3 times, rep from * to end of rnd—168 sts.

RNDS 49 AND 51: Knit.

RND 52: *[Yo, k1] 4 times, ssk 3 times, k2tog 3 times, [k1, yo] 4 times, k1; rep from * to end of rnd—184 sts.

RNDS 53–56: Knit.

RND 57: *[Yo, k1] 5 times, ssk 3 times, k2tog 3 times, [k1, yo] 5 times, k1; rep from * to end of rnd—216 sts.

RNDS 58–61: Knit.

RND 62: *Yo, [k1, yo] 5 times, ssk 4 times, k2tog 4 times, [yo, k1] 6 times; rep from * to end of rnd—248 sts.

RND 63: Knit.

SHAPE ARMHOLES

RND 1: K31, BO 31 sts very loosely for armhole, k124, BO 31 sts very loosely for armhole, k31.

RND 2: K31; with backward-loop method (see Glossary), CO 31 sts very loosely, k124, CO 31 sts very loosely, k31.

RND 3: Knit.

RND 4: *Yo, [k1, yo] 5 times, k2, ssk 4 times, k2tog 4 times, k2, [yo, k1] 6 times; rep from * to end of rnd—280 sts.

RNDS 5–8: Knit.

RND 9: *Yo, [k1, yo] 6 times, k1, ssk 5 times, k2tog 5 times, [k1, yo] 7 times, k1; rep from * to end of rnd—312 sts.

RNDS 10–13: Knit.

RND 14: *Yo, [k1, yo] 7 times, ssk 6 times, k2tog 6 times, [yo, k1] 8 times; rep from * to end of rnd—344 sts.

RNDS 15–18: Knit.

RND 19: *Yo, [k1, yo] 7 times, k2,

ssk 6 times, k2tog 6 times, k2, [yo, k1] 8 times; rep from * to end of rnd—376 sts.

RNDS 20–23: Knit.

Place last 47 sts of Rnd 23 and first 46 sts of rnd on separate holders; place center 93 sts on a third holder—95 sts rem on each side for fronts. Work each side of the front separately.

SHAPE FRONT

Row 24: (RS) K1, *yo, [k1, yo] 7 times, ssk 8 times, k2tog 8 times, [yo, k1] 8 times, rep from * 2 times, [turn work and purl to last 4 sts, turn work and knit to the last 4 sts] 2 times.

Row 25: (WS) [P1, yo] 4 times, [p2tog, p1] 4 times, p2tog tbl 8 times, yo, [p1, yo] 15 times, p2tog 8 times, [p1, p2tog tbl] 4 times, yo, [p1, yo] 3 times, p1, [turn work and knit to last 4 sts, turn work and purl to last 4 sts] 2 times.

Row 26: (RS) K8, k2tog 8 times, yo, [k1, yo] 15 times, ssk 8 times, k8, [turn work and purl to last 4 sts, turn work and knit to last 4 sts] 2 times.

Row 27: (WS) [P2tog tbl] 8 times, yo, [p1, yo] 15 times, p2tog 8 times, [turn work and knit to last 4 sts, turn work and purl to last 4 sts] 2 times. Place sts on a holder.

Attach yarn to the other side and rep Rows 24–27.

EDGING

Replace all sts on size 9 (10) cir needles and resume working in the rnd. Work 4 rnds in garter st. BO all sts very loosely knitwise.

SLEEVES

With size 9 (10) dpns and a double strand of yarn, CO 54 sts loosely. Cut one strand. Knit 4 rows.

Change to short cir and join to work in the rnd, being careful not to twist sts, and pm at beg of rnd.

RNDS 1 AND 2: Knit.

RND 3: *K2tog 3 times, [yo, k1] 6 times, ssk 3 times; rep from * to end of rnd.

RND 4: Knit.

Rep Rnds 1–4 and *at the same time* inc 1 st at each side of marker for under-arm when sleeve measures 4", 6", 8", and 9¾" (10, 15, 20, and 25 cm), working new sts in stockinette—62 sts.

When sleeve measures about 17 (18)" (43 [45.5] cm), work Rows 1–4 back and forth in patt (see below) and *at the same time* BO 2 sts at beg of next 26 rows.

Row 1: (RS) Knit.

Row 2: (WS) Purl.

Row 3: (RS) *K2tog 3 times, [yo, k1] 6 times, ssk 3 times; rep from * to end of rnd.

Row 4: (WS) Purl.

BO rem 10 sts.

FINISHING

Fold CO sts for armhole up toward shoulder and sew to corresponding BO sleeve cap sts. (Join one shoulder first and make sure that the sleeve cap fits into the armhole before you sew the seams.) Sew remaining portion of sleeve in place.

lace circle sweater

aran TURTLENECK

This classic sweater has a few feminine twists. The set-in sleeves and waist shaping give the traditional Aran a more figure-flattering shape, and the modern leaf pattern makes this a sweater you'll be happy to wear for years.

FINISHED MEASUREMENTS
36¼ (38½, 41, 43¼)" (92 [98, 104, 110] cm) bust circumference; 22 (22¾, 23¾, 24½)" (56 [58, 60, 62] cm) long.

YARN
DK weight (Light #3).
Shown here: Sandnesgarn Peer Gynt (100% wool; 100 yd [91 m]/50 g]): natural, 14 (15, 16, 17) balls. See page 126 for yarn substitution suggestions.

NEEDLES
U.S. size 2 (3 mm) and U.S. size 6 (4 mm): straight. U.S. size 2 (3 mm): 26" (40 cm) circular. Adjust needle sizes if necessary to obtain the correct gauge.

NOTIONS
Tapestry needle.

GAUGE
21 sts and 29 rows = 4" (10 cm) in stockinette stitch on larger needles.

NOTE
Work the first and last stitch of every row in garter stitch (knit on RS and WS).

BACK

With smaller needles, CO 113 (121, 129, 137) sts.

Row 1: (WS) K2, [p1, k3] to last 3 sts, p1, k2.

Work in ribbing as established (working sts as they appear) and *at the same time* work the first and last st of each row as k1 for a garter st edge. Work in ribbing until piece measures 1½" (4 cm), ending after a RS row.

Next row: (WS) K2, *[p1, k3] 3 times, p1, k2tog, k1; rep from * 5 (6, 6, 7) more times, [p1, k3] 3 (1, 3, 1) time(s), p1, k2—107 (114, 122, 129) sts.

Work sts in patt as established until piece measures 2¾" (7 cm), ending after a RS row.

Next row: (WS) K2, *[p1, k3] 2 times, p1, k2tog, k1, [p1, k2]; rep from * 5 (6, 6, 7) more times, [p1, k3, p1] 3 (1, 3, 1) time(s), p1, k2—101 (107, 115, 121) sts.

Work even in patt until piece measures 4" (10 cm), ending after a RS row.

Next row: (WS) K2, *p1, k3, p1, k2tog, k1, [p1, k2] 2 times; rep from * 5 (6, 6, 7) more times, [p1, k3, p1] 3 (1, 3, 1) time(s), p1, k2—95 (100, 108, 113) sts.

Work even in patt until piece measures 5¼" (13 cm), ending after a RS row.

Next row: (WS) K2, *p1, k2tog, k1, [p1, k2] 3 times; rep from * 5 (6, 6, 7) more times, [p1, k2tog, k1] 3 (1, 3, 1) time(s), p1, k2—86 (92, 98, 104) sts rem.

Continue in patt until piece measures 5½" (14 cm), ending after a RS row.

Next row: (WS) Work in established

rib patt and *at the same time* inc 7 sts evenly spaced across row—93 (99, 105, 111) sts. Change to larger needles.

NEXT ROW: (RS) K1, p0 (3, 6, 9), work Row 1 of Aran chart across 91 sts, p0 (3, 6, 9), k1.

Work in patt (working each edge st in garter st, side sts in reverse St st, and continue Aran chart over center 91 sts) and *at the same time* k1f&b one st from each edge when piece measures 7", 8¾", 10¼", 11¾", and 13⅓" (18, 22, 26, 30, and 34 cm), working inc'd sts in reverse St st—103 (109, 115, 121) sts. Cont in established patts until piece measures 14¼ (14½, 15, 15½)" (36 [37, 38, 39] cm), ending after a WS row.

SHAPE ARMHOLES

BO 3 sts at beg of next 2 rows, 2 sts at beg of next 4 rows, 1 (2, 2, 2) st(s) at beg of next 2 rows, 1 (1, 1, 2) st(s) at beg of next 2 rows, and 1 st at beg of next 4 rows—81 (85, 91, 95) sts rem.

LARGEST SIZE ONLY

BO 1 st at beg of next 2 rows—93 sts rem. Work even in established patts until armhole measures 7½ (8, 8¼, 8¾)" (19 [20, 21, 22] cm), ending after a WS row.

SHAPE NECK AND SHOULDERS (ALL SIZES)

NEXT ROW: (RS) Work in patt across 23 (24, 26, 27) sts, place the center 35 (37, 39, 39) sts on a holder for neck, join a new ball of yarn and work in patt across rem

23 (24, 26, 27) sts. Working each side separately, BO 7 (8, 8, 9) sts at beg of next 2 rows, then BO 8 (8, 9, 9) sts at beg of next 2 rows, then BO rem 8 (8, 9, 9) sts.

FRONT

Work as for back until armholes measure 2½ (2¾, 3¼, 3½)" (6 [7, 8, 9] cm), ending after a WS row—81 (85, 91, 93) sts.

NEXT ROW: (RS) Work in patt across 33 (34, 36, 37) sts, place center 15 (17, 19, 19) sts on a holder for neck, join a new ball of yarn and work in patt across rem 33 (34, 36, 37) sts. Working each side separately, BO 3 sts at neck edge once, 2 sts twice, and 1 st 3 times—23 (24, 26, 27) sts rem.

When front is same length as back to shoulders, BO 7 (8, 8, 9) sts at shoulder edge once, then BO 8 (8, 9, 9) sts at shoulder edge once, then BO 8 (8, 9, 9) rem sts.

SLEEVES

With smaller needles, CO 62 (62, 65, 65) sts.

NEXT ROW: (WS) K2, [p1, k2] to end.

Work ribbing as established, keeping first and last sts of each row in garter st, until sleeve measures 3¼" (8 cm), ending after a RS row.

NEXT ROW: (WS; dec row) K2tog once, cont in established ribbing to last 0 (0, 2, 2) sts, k2tog 0 (0,

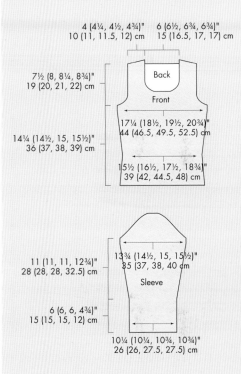

4 (4¼, 4½, 4¾)"
10 (11, 11.5, 12) cm

6 (6½, 6¾, 6¾)"
15 (16.5, 17, 17) cm

7½ (8, 8¼, 8¾)"
19 (20, 21, 22) cm

Back

Front

17¼ (18½, 19½, 20¾)"
44 (46.5, 49.5, 52.5) cm

14¼ (14½, 15, 15½)"
36 (37, 38, 39) cm

15½ (16½, 17½, 18¾)"
39 (42, 44.5, 48) cm

11 (11, 11, 12¾)"
28 (28, 28, 32.5) cm

13¾ (14½, 15, 15½)"
35 (37, 38, 40 cm

Sleeve

6 (6, 6, 4¾)"
15 (15, 15, 12) cm

10¼ (10¼, 10¾, 10¾)"
26 (26, 27.5, 27.5) cm

1, 1) time(s)—61 (61, 63, 63) sts rem.

Change to larger needles and work Sleeve chart as indicated for your size, keeping edge sts in garter st (not shown on chart), until piece measures 6 (6, 6, 4¾)" (15 [15, 15, 12] cm), ending after a WS row.
NEXT ROW: (RS; inc row) K1, p1f&b, work chart to last 2 sts, p1f&b, k1—2 sts inc'd.

Cont in patt as established and *at the same time* rep inc row every 1¼ (1, 1, 1)" (3 [2.5, 2.5, 2.5 cm) 8 (10, 10, 11) more times, working inc'd sts into patt —79 (83, 85, 87) sts.

Work even in patt until piece measures 17" (43 cm) or desired length.

SHAPE SLEEVE CAP
BO 3 sts at beg of next 2 rows, 2 (2, 2, 3) sts at beg of next 2 rows, 2 sts at beg of next 2 rows, 1 st at beg of next 12 (14, 16, 16) rows, 2 sts at beg of next 8 rows, 3 sts at beg of next 6 rows, and 4 sts at beg of next 2 rows. BO rem 11 (13, 13, 13) sts.

FINISHING
With yarn threaded on a tapestry needle, sew shoulder seams. With smaller cir, pick up and knit 126 (132, 138, 138) sts evenly around

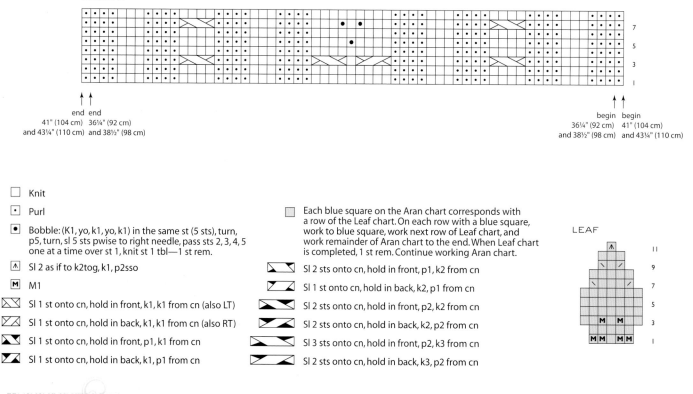

SLEEVE

7
5
3
1

end end
41" (104 cm)   36¼" (92 cm)
and 43¼" (110 cm)   and 38½" (98 cm)

begin begin
36¼" (92 cm)   41" (104 cm)
and 38½" (98 cm)   and 43¼" (110 cm)

☐ Knit

• Purl

● Bobble: (K1, yo, k1, yo, k1) in the same st (5 sts), turn, p5, turn, sl 5 sts pwise to right needle, pass sts 2, 3, 4, 5 one at a time over st 1, knit st 1 tbl—1 st rem.

Λ Sl 2 as if to k2tog, k1, p2sso

M M1

Sl 1 st onto cn, hold in front, k1, k1 from cn (also LT)

Sl 1 st onto cn, hold in back, k1, k1 from cn (also RT)

Sl 1 st onto cn, hold in front, p1, k1 from cn

Sl 1 st onto cn, hold in back, k1, p1 from cn

☐ Each blue square on the Aran chart corresponds with a row of the Leaf chart. On each row with a blue square, work to blue square, work next row of Leaf chart, and work remainder of Aran chart to the end. When Leaf chart is completed, 1 st rem. Continue working Aran chart.

Sl 2 sts onto cn, hold in front, p1, k2 from cn

Sl 1 st onto cn, hold in back, k2, p1 from cn

Sl 2 sts onto cn, hold in front, p2, k2 from cn

Sl 2 sts onto cn, hold in back, k2, p2 from cn

Sl 3 sts onto cn, hold in front, p2, k3 from cn

Sl 2 sts onto cn, hold in back, k3, p2 from cn

LEAF

11
9
7
5
3
1

neck opening. Join for working in the round. Work [k1, p2] until neck measures 2" (5 cm).

NEXT ROW: (turning row) Work sts the opposite of how they appear (i.e., p1, k2 ribbing).

Cont in new ribbing patt until neck measures 4" (10 cm) from pick-up rnd.

NEXT RND: *P1, k2, p1, k1, M1, k1; rep from * to end of rnd.

NEXT RND: *P1, k2, p1, k3; rep from * to end of rnd.

Work ribbing until neck measures 8" (20 cm). BO all sts loosely in patt. Sew in sleeves, then sew underarms and side seams. Weave in ends.

ARAN

JACKET FOR
everyone

This jacket looks good on almost everyone. Stockinette stitch alternates with columns of easy-to-remember lace on the back and sleeves, while the front features intriguing braided cables with lace and bobbles for texture.

FINISHED MEASUREMENTS

36¼ (38½, 41, 43¼)" (92 [98, 104, 110] cm) bust circumference; 22¾ (23¾, 24½, 25¼)" (58 [60, 62, 64] cm) long.

YARN

Worsted (Medium #4).
Shown here: Coats Løve Iceland (50% wool, 35% acrylic, 15% alpaca; 165 yd (150 m)/50 g): #66 aqua, 8 (8, 9, 10) balls. See page 126 for yarn substitution suggestions.

NEEDLES

U.S. size 2 (3 mm) and U.S. size 4 (3.5 mm). Adjust needle sizes if necessary to obtain the correct gauge.

NOTIONS

Tapestry needle; sewing needle and thread; six ½" (1.3 cm) buttons.

GAUGE

19½ sts and 28 rows = 4" (10 cm) in stockinette stitch and lace pattern on larger needles.

NOTE

Work the first and last stitch of every row in garter stitch (knit on RS and WS).

BACK

RIBBING

With smaller needles, CO 113 (119, 125, 131) sts.

Row 1: (WS) K2, [p1, k2] to end.

Row 2: K1, p1, k1, [p2, k1] to last 2 sts, p1, k1.

Rep Rows 1 and 2 for patt until piece measures ¾" (2 cm), ending after a WS row.

Next row: (RS; dec row) K1, k2tog or p2tog to maintain patt, [p2, k1] to last 3 sts, k2tog or p2tog to maintain patt, k1—2 sts dec'd.

Work in patt and *at the same time* rep dec row when piece measures 2" (5 cm) and 3¼" (8 cm)—107 (113, 119, 125) sts rem.

Cont even in patt until piece measures 4" (10 cm), ending after a RS row.

Next row: (WS) Work in patt as established, working k2tog in every other rep of [p1, k2], until 19 (19, 20, 20) sts have been dec'd—88 (94, 99, 105) sts rem.

LACE

With larger needles, work in stockinette and lace as foll:

Row 1: (RS) K1 (edge st), k3 (6, 3, 6), work Lace chart once, *k8, work Lace chart on 3 sts; rep from * to last 4 (7, 4, 7) sts, k3 (6, 3, 5), k1 (edge st).

Work in patt as established until piece measures 4½" (11.5 cm) from beg, ending after a WS row.

Next row: (RS, dec row) K1, k2tog, work in patt to last 3 sts, k2tog, k1—2 sts dec'd.

Work in patt and *at the same time* rep dec row when piece measures 5½" (14 cm) from CO—84 (90, 95, 101) sts rem.

Cont in patt until piece measures 8" (20 cm) from CO, ending after a WS row.

Next row: (RS; inc row) K1, M1 (see Glossary), work in patt to last st, M1, k1—2 sts inc'd.

Work in patt and *at the same time* rep inc row when piece measures 10¼", 12¾", and 15" (26, 32, and 38 cm) from beg—92 (98, 103, 109) sts.

Work even in patt until piece measures 15 (15½, 15¾, 16¼)" (38 [39, 40, 41] cm) from CO.

SHAPE ARMHOLES

Cont in patt as established, shape armholes by binding off as foll: BO 3 sts at beg of next 2 rows, BO 2 (2, 3, 3) sts at beg of next 2 rows, BO 2 sts at beg of next 2 rows, BO 1 (2, 2, 2) st(s) at beg of next 2 rows, BO 1 (1, 1, 2) st(s) at beg of next 2 rows, BO 1 st at beg of next 2 rows, BO 0 (1, 1, 1) st(s) at beg of next 2 rows—72 (74, 77, 81) sts rem.

Work even in patt until armhole measures 7½ (8, 8¼, 8¾)" (19 [20, 21, 22] cm), ending after a WS row.

Next row: (RS) K18 (19, 20, 21), join another ball of yarn, work center 36 (36, 37, 39) sts on a holder for neck, k18 (19, 20, 21).

Working each side separately, BO 6 sts at each shoulder edge 3 (2, 1, 0) time(s), then BO 7 sts at each shoulder edge 0 (1, 2, 3) time(s).

RIGHT FRONT

RIBBING

With smaller needles, CO 59 (62, 65, 68) sts and work in ribbing as for back until piece measures ¾" (2 cm), ending after a WS row.

Next row: (RS; dec row) Work in patt to last 3 sts, k2tog (or p2tog) maintaining patt, k1—2 sts dec'd.

Work in patt and *at the same time* rep dec row when piece measures 2" (5 cm) and 3¼" (8 cm)—56 (59, 62, 65) sts rem.

Cont even in patt until piece measures 4" (10 cm), ending after a RS row.

Next row: (WS; dec row) Work in patt as established, working k2tog in every other rep of [p1, k2] until 4 (4, 5, 5) sts have been dec'd—52 (55, 57, 60) sts rem.

LACE

With larger needles, work Right Front chart for appropriate size, maintaining garter st edges (not shown on chart).

SIZE M ONLY

Omit outermost yo at side seam because there aren't enough sts for the complete lace motif; work those sts in stockinette instead.

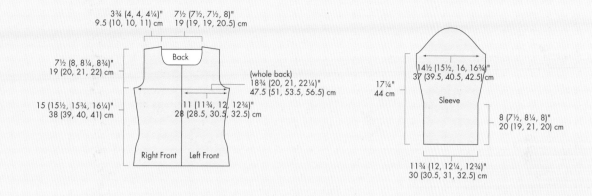

ALL SIZES

Work in patt as established until piece measures 4½" (11.5 cm) from CO, ending after a WS row.

NEXT ROW: (RS; dec row) Work in patt to last 3 sts, k2tog, k1—1 st dec'd.

Work in patt and *at the same time* rep dec row when piece measures 5½" (14 cm) from CO—50 (53, 55, 58) sts rem.

Cont in patt until piece measures 8" (20 cm) from CO, ending after a WS row.

NEXT ROW: (RS; inc row) Work in patt to last st, M1, k1—1 st inc'd.

Work in patt and *at the same time* rep inc row when piece measures 10¼", 12¾", and 15" (26, 32, and 38 cm) from CO—54 (57, 59, 62) sts.

Work even in patt until piece measures 15 (15½, 15¾, 16¼)" (38 [39, 40, 41] cm) from CO.

SHAPE ARMHOLE AND NECK

Cont in patt as established, shape armhole by binding off as foll: BO at armhole edge (beg of WS row): 3 sts 1 (1, 2, 2) time(s), 2 sts 3 (4, 3, 3) times, 1 st 3 (2, 2, 3) times—42 (44, 45, 47) sts rem.

Work in patt until armhole measures 4¾ (5¼, 5½, 6)" (12 [13, 14, 15] cm), ending after a WS row.

NEXT ROW: (RS) BO 12 (13, 13, 14) sts (neck edge), work in patt to end.

Cont in patt, BO at neck edge every other row 3 sts 1 time, 2 sts 3 times, 1 st 3 times—18 (19, 20, 21) sts rem. When piece measures the same as for back, shape shoulder as for back.

LEFT FRONT

RIBBING

With smaller needles, CO 59 (62, 65, 68) sts and work in ribbing as for back until piece measures ¾" (2 cm), ending after a WS row.

NEXT ROW: (RS; dec row) K1, k2tog (or p2tog) maintaining patt, work in patt to last st, k1—1 st dec'd.

Work in patt and *at the same time* rep dec row when piece measures 2" (5 cm) and 3¼" (8 cm)—56 (59, 62, 65) sts rem.

Cont even in patt until piece measures 4" (10 cm), ending after a RS row.

NEXT ROW: (WS; dec row) Work in patt as established, working k2tog in every other rep of [p1, k2] until 4 (4, 5, 5) sts have been dec'd—52 (55, 57, 60) sts rem.

LACE

With larger needles, work Left Front chart for appropriate size, maintaining garter st edges (not shown on chart).

RIGHT FRONT

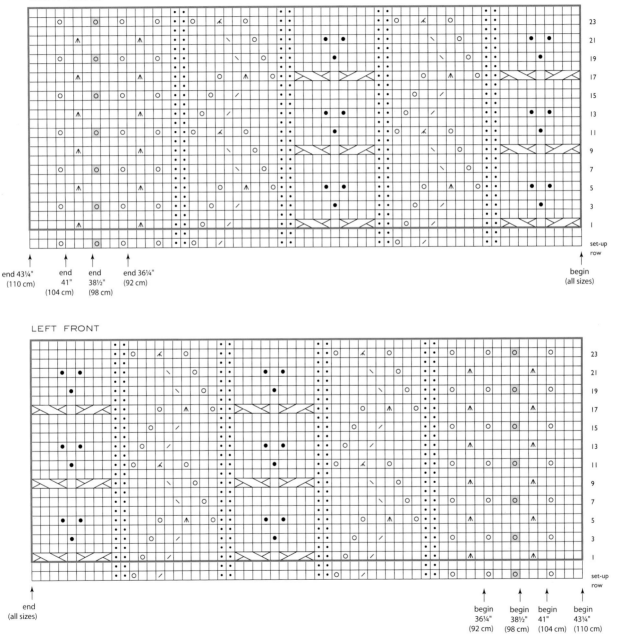

end 43¼"
(110 cm)

end
41"
(104 cm)

end
38½"
(98 cm)

end 36¼"
(92 cm)

begin
(all sizes)

set-up
row

LEFT FRONT

end
(all sizes)

begin
36¼"
(92 cm)

begin
38½"
(98 cm)

begin
41"
(104 cm)

begin
43¼"
(110 cm)

set-up
row

SIZE M ONLY

Omit outermost yo at side seam because there aren't enough sts for the complete lace motif; work those sts in stockinette instead.

ALL SIZES

Work in patt as established until piece measures 4½" (11.5 cm) from CO, ending after a WS row.

NEXT ROW: (RS; dec row) K1, k2tog, work in patt to last st, k1—1 st dec'd.

Work in patt and *at the same time* rep dec row when piece measures 5½" (14 cm) from CO—50 (53, 55, 58) sts rem.

Cont in patt until piece measures 8" (20 cm) from CO, ending after a WS row.

NEXT ROW: (RS; inc row) K1, M1, work in patt to last st, k1—1 st inc'd.

Work in patt and *at the same time* rep inc row when piece measures 10¼", 12¾", and 15" (26, 32, and 38 cm) from CO—54 (57, 59, 62) sts.

Work even in patt until piece measures 15 (15½, 15¾, 16¼)" (38 [39, 40, 41] cm) from CO.

SHAPE ARMHOLE AND NECK

Cont in patt as established, shape armhole by binding off as foll: BO at armhole edge (beg of RS row) 3 sts 1 (1, 2, 2) time(s), 2 sts 3 (4, 3, 3) times, 1 st 3 (2, 2, 3) times—42 (44, 45, 47) sts rem.

Work in patt until armhole measures 4¾ (5¼, 5½, 6)" (12 [13, 14, 15] cm), ending after a RS row.

NEXT ROW: (WS) BO 12 (13, 13, 14) sts (neck edge), work in patt to end.

LACE

3

1

	Knit on RS; purl on WS
	Purl on RS; knit on WS
	Yarnover
	Yarnover *except for 38½" (98 cm)* work in St st to maintain stitch count
	Sl 2 as if to k2tog, k1, p2sso
	Knit into front, back, front of same st
	K3tog
	Sl 1, k2tog, psso

	Bobble: (K1, p1, k1, p1, k1) into the same st (5 sts), turn, p5, turn, sl 5 sts pwise to right needle, pass sts 2, 3, 4, 5 one at a time over st 1, knit st 1 tbl—1 st rem.
	K2tog
	Ssk
	Sl 2 sts onto cn, hold in front, k2, k2 from cn
	Sl 2 sts onto cn, hold in back, k2, k2 from cn
	No stitch
	Pattern repeat

Cont in patt, BO at neck edge every other row 3 sts 1 time, 2 sts 3 times, 1 st 3 times—18 (19, 20, 21) sts rem. When piece measures the same as for back, shape armhole as for back.

SLEEVES

RIBBING

With smaller needles, CO 71 (74, 77, 77) sts. Work ribbing as for back for 4" (10 cm), ending after a RS row.

Row 1: (WS) K2tog, *p1, k2tog; rep from * 13 (14, 14, 14) times—57 (59, 62, 62) sts rem.

LACE

With larger needles, work stockinette and lace pattern as foll:

Row 1: (RS) K5 (6, 1, 2), work Row 1 of Arm chart, *k8, rep Row 1 of Arm chart; work from * to last 5 (6, 1, 2) st(s), knit to end.

Cont in St st and Lace patt as established until piece measures 8 (7½, 8¼, 8)" (20 [19, 21, 20] cm), ending after a WS row.

Next row: (RS; inc row) K1, M1, work in patt to last st, M, k1—2 sts inc'd.

Cont in patt as established, working new sts into St st and *at the same time* rep inc row every 1¼ (1¼, 1, ¾)" (3 [3, 2.5, 2] cm) 6 (7, 8, 9) more times—69 (73, 78, 80) sts.

Cont even in patt until piece measures 17¼" (44 cm) or desired length.

SHAPE SLEEVE CAP

BO 2 sts at beg of next 2 rows, BO 2 (2, 3, 3) sts at beg of next 2 rows, BO 2 sts at beg of next 2 rows, BO 1 st at beg of next 14 (16, 18, 18) rows, BO 2 sts at beg of next 8 rows, 3 sts at beg of next 4 rows, BO 4 sts at beg of next 2 rows, BO rem 7 (9, 10, 12) sts.

FINISHING

With yarn threaded on a tapestry needle, sew shoulder seams.

LEFT FRONT EDGE

With smaller needles, pick up and knit 107 (113, 121, 127) sts (about 3 sts for every 4 rows) along left front edge. Work in ribbing as above for 1" (2.5 cm). BO in patt.

RIGHT FRONT EDGE

Pick up and knit 107 (113, 121, 127) sts along right front band. Work in ribbing for ³⁄₈" (1 cm).

NEXT ROW: (buttonhole row) Maintaining rib patt, work 3 (6, 3, 6) sts, *BO 2 sts, work ribbing for 19 (19, 24, 24) sts; rep from * 3 more times, BO 2 sts, work 18 (21, 12, 15) sts.

Use the backward-loop method (see Glossary) to CO 2 new sts over gaps to complete buttonholes on next row. *Note:* The fifth buttonhole will be made at center top of neckband.

Cont in ribbing until band measures 1" (2.5 cm). BO in patt.

NECKBAND

With smaller needles, pick up and knit about 106 (109, 112, 115) sts around neck (about 3 sts every 4 rows) beginning at right front, along right front edge, across back neck inc 1 st about every 5 sts, then along left front edge. Work in k1, p2 ribbing for 1" (2.5 cm), making a buttonhole (BO 2 sts) in neckband after ³⁄₈" (1 cm), aligned with other buttonholes. BO in ribbing.

With sewing needle and thread, sew buttons on left front edging to correspond with buttonholes. With yarn threaded on a tapestry needle, sew sleeves into armholes. Sew sleeve and side seams.

flower JACKET

Usually lace is worked against a stockinette background, but this short-sleeve jacket turns the tables. It features a stockinette flower motif against an open, lacy background. With short sleeves and an open pattern, it's perfect for a summer evening.

FINISHED MEASUREMENTS
33 (36, 38½, 41¼)" (84 [91, 98, 105] cm) bust circumference; 16½ (17¼, 18¼, 19)" (42 [44, 46, 48] cm) length.

YARN
DK weight (Light #3)
Shown here: Coats Løve Siesta (50% viscose, 50% acrylic; 126 yd [115 m]/50 g): #66 aqua, 6 (6, 7, 8) balls. See page 126 for yarn substitution suggestions.

NEEDLES
U.S. size 2 (3 mm) and U.S. size 4 (3.5 mm). Adjust needle size if necessary to obtain the correct gauge.

NOTIONS
Tapestry needle; sewing needle and thread; four ¾" (2 cm) buttons.

GAUGE
23 sts and 27 rows = 4" (10 cm) in lace patt on larger needles.

NOTE
Work the first and last stitch of every row in garter stitch (knit on RS and WS).

BACK

With smaller needles, CO 91 (99, 107, 115) sts. Knit 7 rows.

Change to larger needles. Work in Lace chart, working first and last sts of each row in garter st (not shown on chart), until piece measures 2½" (6 cm) from CO, ending with a WS row.

NEXT ROW: (RS; inc row) K1, M1 (see Glossary), work in patt to last st, M1, k1—2 sts inc'd.

Cont even in patt, working new sts into lace patt and *at the same time* rep inc row every 2" (5 cm) 4 more times—99 (107, 115, 123) sts. *Note:* If there are not enough sts to complete paired decs and yos, omit yos or work St st without decs.

Cont in patt until piece measures 8¾ (9, 9¾, 10¼)" (22 [23, 25, 26] cm) from CO.

SHAPE ARMHOLES

BO 3 sts at beg of next 2 rows, BO 2 sts at beg of next 4 rows, BO 1 (1, 2, 2) st(s) at beg of next 2 rows, BO 1 st at beg of next 2 rows, BO 0 (1, 1, 1) st(s) at beg of next 2 rows—81 (87, 93, 101) sts rem.

LARGEST SIZE ONLY

BO 1 st at beg of next 2 rows—99 sts rem.

ALL SIZES

Work even in patt until armhole measures 2½ (2¾, 3½, 3½)" (6 [7, 8, 9] cm), ending after a WS row.

NEXT ROW: (RS) Work in patt across 25 (28, 31, 34) sts, work Flower chart over the center 31 sts, work in patt across 25 (28, 31, 34) sts.

Cont in patt as established to end of Flower chart. After completing flower motif, work patt A over all sts until armhole measures 7 (7½, 7½, 8)" (18 [19, 19, 20] cm), ending after a WS row.

NEXT ROW: (RS) Work in patt across 25 (28, 30, 33) sts, BO the center 31 (31, 33, 33) sts for neck, work in patt across 25 (28, 30, 33) sts. Working each side separately, at armhole edge, BO 8 (9, 10, 11) sts twice, then BO rem 9 (10, 10, 11) sts.

LEFT FRONT

With smaller needles, CO 51 (55, 59, 63) sts. Knit 7 rows. Change to larger needles.

ROW 1: (RS) K1 (side seam edge),

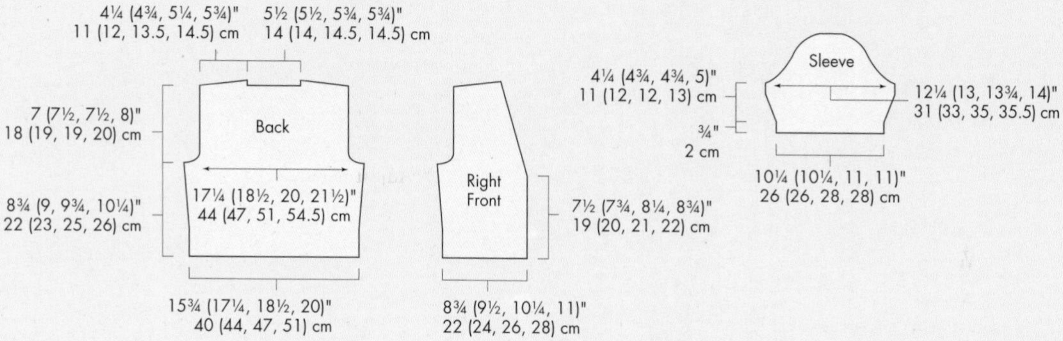

Back

4¼ (4¾, 5¼, 5¾)"
11 (12, 13.5, 14.5) cm

5½ (5½, 5¾, 5¾)"
14 (14, 14.5, 14.5) cm

7 (7½, 7½, 8)"
18 (19, 19, 20) cm

8¾ (9, 9¾, 10¼)"
22 (23, 25, 26) cm

17¼ (18½, 20, 21½)"
44 (47, 51, 54.5) cm

15¾ (17¼, 18½, 20)"
40 (44, 47, 51) cm

Right Front

8¾ (9½, 10¼, 11)"
22 (24, 26, 28) cm

7½ (7¾, 8¼, 8¾)"
19 (20, 21, 22) cm

Sleeve

4¼ (4¾, 4¾, 5)"
11 (12, 12, 13) cm

¾"
2 cm

12¼ (13, 13¾, 14)"
31 (33, 35, 35.5) cm

10¼ (10¼, 11, 11)"
26 (26, 28, 28) cm

work Lace chart to last 5 sts, k5 (front edge).

Rows 2–12 (14, 16, 14): Cont in chart, keeping outermost st at the side seam and outermost 5 sts at front edge in garter st.

Row 13 (15, 17, 15): (RS) K1 (side seam edge), work 9 (11, 13, 15) sts in patt A, work Row 1 of Flower chart over 31 sts, work Lace chart across 5 (7, 9, 11) sts, k5 (front edge).

Cont in patt as established until piece measures 2½" (6 cm), ending with a WS row.

Next row: (RS; inc row) K1, M1, work in patt to end—1 st inc'd.

Cont even in patt, working new sts into lace patt and *at the same time* rep inc row every 2" (5 cm) 3 more times—55 (59, 63, 67) sts. *Note:* If there are not enough sts to complete paired decs and yos, omit yos or work St st without decs.

Cont in patt to end of Flower chart.

Next row: (RS) K1, work Lace chart to last 5 sts, k5.

Cont in patt as established until piece measures 7½ (8, 8¼, 8¾)" (19 [20, 21, 22] cm), ending after a WS row.

SHAPE NECKLINE

Next row: (RS) Work in patt to last 7 sts, ssk, k5—1 st dec'd.

Rep dec row every 4th row and *at the same time* dec for armhole as for back when piece measures 8¾ (9, 9¾, 10¼)" (22 [23, 25, 26] cm).

LACE

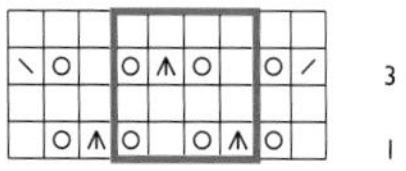

FLOWER

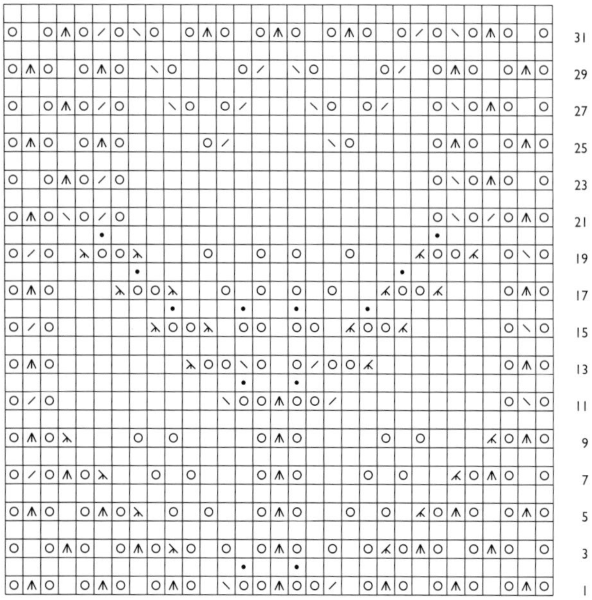

- ☐ Knit on RS; purl on WS
- ⊡ Purl on RS; knit on WS
- ⊙ Yarnover
- ∕ K2tog
- ∖ Ssk
- ⅄ Sssk
- ⊿ K3tog
- ⋀ Sl 2 as if to k2tog, k1, p2sso
- ☐ Pattern repeat

After armhole shaping is complete, continue to dec at neck edge until 30 (33, 35, 38) sts rem.

When armhole measures 7 (7½, 7½, 8)" (18 [19, 19, 20] cm), BO 8 (9, 10, 11) sts at armhole edge (beg of RS rows) twice, then BO 9 (10, 10, 11) sts at beg of next RS row—5 sts rem.

Place rem 5 sts on a holder for front band. Mark placement of 4 buttons on left front band: top button just below lowest dec for V-neck, bottom button ⅜" (1 cm) from lower edge, and rem 2 buttons evenly spaced between.

RIGHT FRONT

Work as for left front, reversing shaping and making buttonholes on band.

With smaller needles, CO 51 (55, 59, 63) sts. Knit 7 rows.

Change to larger needles.

ROW 1: (RS) K5 (front edge), work patt A to last st, k1 (side seam).

ROWS 2–12 (14, 16, 14): Cont in Lace chart, keeping outermost st at the side seam and outermost 5 sts at front edge in garter st.

ROW 13 (15, 17, 15): (RS) K5, work 5 (7, 9, 11) sts following Lace chart, work Row 1 of Flower chart over 31 sts, work in Lace patt to last st, k1. Cont in patt as established until piece measures 2½" (6 cm), ending with a WS row.

NEXT ROW: (RS; inc row) Work in patt to last st, M1, k1—1 st inc'd. Cont even in patt, working new sts into lace patt and *at the same time* rep inc row every 2" (5 cm) 3 more times—55 (59, 63, 67) sts. *Note:* If there are not enough sts to complete paired decs and yos, omit yos or work St st without decs.

Cont in patt to end of Flower chart.

NEXT ROW: (RS) K5, work Lace chart to last st, k1.

Cont in patt until piece measures 7½ (8, 8¼, 8¾)" (19 [20, 21, 22] cm), ending after a WS row.

SHAPE NECKLINE
NEXT ROW: (RS) K5 (front edge), k2tog, work to end as established. Rep dec row every 4th row, working buttonholes spaced as for buttons (k2 from front edge, yo, k2tog, k1) and *at the same time* dec for armhole as for back when piece measures 8¾ (9, 9¾, 10¼)" (22 [23, 25, 26] cm). After armhole shaping is complete, continue to dec at neck edge until 30 (33, 35, 38) sts rem.

When armhole measures 7 (7½, 7½, 8)" (18 [19, 19, 20] cm), BO 8 (9, 10, 11) sts at beg of next 2 RS rows, then BO 9 (10, 10, 11) sts at beg of next RS row—5 sts rem. Place rem 5 sts on a holder for front band.

SLEEVES

With smaller needles, CO 59 (59, 63, 63) sts. Knit 7 rows.

Change to larger needles.
Work in Lace chart, working first and last sts of each row in garter st, beginning and ending as indicated on chart until piece measures ¾" (2 cm) from CO, ending with a WS row.

NEXT ROW: (RS; inc row) K1, M1, work in patt to last st, M1, k1—2 sts inc'd.

Cont in patt as established, rep inc row every ½ (⅜, ⅜, ⅜)" (1.3 [1, 3, 1] cm) 5 (7, 7, 8) more times working inc sts into patt —71 (75, 79, 81) sts.

Cont in patt until piece measures 4¼ (4¾, 4¾, 5)" (11 [12, 12, 13] cm).

SHAPE SLEEVE CAP
BO 3 sts at beg of next 2 rows, BO 2 (2, 3, 2) sts at beg of next 2 rows, BO 2 sts at beg of next 2 rows—57 (61, 63, 67) sts rem.

LARGEST SIZE ONLY
BO 2 sts at beg of next 2 rows—63 sts rem.

ALL SIZES
BO 1 st at beg of next 12 (14, 16, 16) rows, BO 2 sts at beg of next 6 rows, BO 3 sts at beg of next 4 rows, BO 4 sts at beg of next 2 rows, BO rem 13 (15, 15, 15) sts.

FINISHING

With yarn threaded on a tapestry needle, sew shoulder seams.

Place left front band sts from holder onto smaller needles and CO 1 edge st at neck. Work in garter st until band reaches center back neck without stretching. Place sts on a holder. Rep for held sts from right front band. With RS of right and left front band sts tog, use three-needle method (see Glossary) to BO sts.

Sew band to back neck. Sew in sleeves. Sew sleeve and side seams.

With sewing needle and thread, sew buttons to left front band to correspond with buttonholes. Weave in ends.

blackberries
& RIBBONS *cardigan*

The small bobble pattern used in this sweater is called blackberries. The simple silhouette is embellished with a narrow ribbon and four large buttons.

FINISHED MEASUREMENTS
35½ (38½, 41¾, 44)" (90 [98, 106, 112] cm) bust circumference; 19 (19¾, 20½, 21¼)" (48 [50, 52, 54] cm) long.

YARN
Worsted weight (Medium #4). *Shown here:* Coats HP Løve Rustico (55% acrylic, 45% cotton; 109 yd [100 m]/50 g): #56 dove blue, 11, (12, 13, 14) balls. See page 126 for yarn substitution suggestions.

NEEDLES
U.S. size 6 (4 mm) and U.S. size 10 (6 mm). Adjust needle sizes if necessary to obtain the correct gauge.

NOTIONS
Tapestry needle; sewing needle and thread; 4 pins; four 1" (2.5 cm) buttons; about 2 yd (2 m) of ³⁄₈" (8 mm) ribbon.

GAUGE
20 sts and 24 rows = 4" (10 cm) in Blackberry pattern.

NOTE
Work the first and last stitch of every row in garter stitch (knit on RS and WS).

stitch guide

BLACKBERRY PATTERN
(multiple of 4 sts plus 2 garter edge sts)
Row 1: (RS) K1, purl to last st, k1.
Row 2: K1, *knit into (front, back, front)
  of next st, p3tog; rep from * to last st, k1.
Row 3: Rep Row 1.
Row 4: K1, *p3tog, knit into (front, back,
  front) of next st; rep from * to last st, k1.
Rep Rows 1–4 for pattern.

BACK

With smaller needles, CO 89 (98, 107, 113) sts.
Row 1: (WS) K2, [p1, k2] to end.
Row 2: K1, p1, k1, [p2, k1] to last 3 sts, p1, k1.
Rep Rows 1 and 2 until ribbing measures 1½" (4 cm), ending after a RS row.
Next row: (WS) Work in patt as established and *at the same time* inc 1 (inc 0, dec 1, inc 1)—90 (98, 106, 114) sts.
Change to larger needles and work Blackberry patt (see Stitch Guide) until piece measures 3¼" (8 cm), ending after a WS row.
Next row: (RS; dec row) K1, p2tog, work in patt to last 3 sts, p2tog, k1—2 sts dec'd.
Cont in patt as established and *at the same time* rep dec row when piece measures 4¼" (11 cm) and 5½" (14 cm)—84 (92, 100, 108) sts rem.

Cont in patt as established until piece measures 7" (18 cm), ending after a WS row.
Next row: (RS; inc row) K1, M1 (see Glossary), work in patt to end, M1, k1—2 sts inc'd.
Cont in patt as established and *at the same time* rep inc row when piece measures 8¾" (22 cm) and 10¼" (26 cm)—90 (98, 106, 114) sts.
Cont even in patt until piece measures 11 (11½, 11¾, 12¼)" (28 [29, 30, 31] cm).

SHAPE ARMHOLES
BO 3 sts at beg of next 2 rows, BO 2 (3, 3, 3) sts at beg of next 2 rows, BO 2 sts at beg of next 2 rows, BO 1 (1, 1, 2) st(s) at beg of next 4 rows, BO 1 st at beg of next 2 (4, 4, 4) rows—70 (74, 82, 86) sts rem.
Continue in patt until armhole measures 7½ (8, 8¼, 8¾)" (19 [20, 21, 22] cm), ending after a WS row.

SHAPE NECK AND SHOULDERS
Next row: (RS row) Work in patt across 17 (19, 22, 23) sts, join another ball of yarn and BO center 36 (36, 38, 40) sts, work in patt across rem 17 (19, 22, 23) sts.
Working each side separately, BO 5 (6, 7, 7) sts once, then BO 6 (6, 7, 7) sts once, then BO 6 (7, 8, 9) rem sts.

LEFT FRONT

With smaller needles, CO 44 (47, 53, 56) sts.
Row 1: (WS) K2, [p1, k2] to end.
Row 2: K1, p1, k1, [p2, k1] to last 2 sts, p1, k1.
Rep Rows 1 and 2 until ribbing measures 1½" (4 cm), ending after a RS row.
Next row: (WS) Work in patt as established and *at the same time*

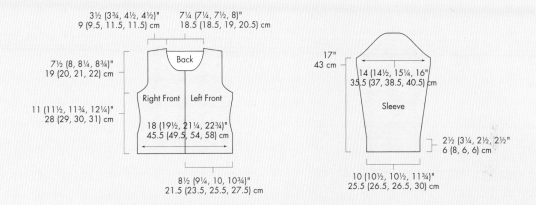

Back

3½ (3¾, 4½, 4½)"
9 (9.5, 11.5, 11.5) cm

7¼ (7¼, 7½, 8)"
18.5 (18.5, 19, 20.5) cm

7½ (8, 8¼, 8¾)"
19 (20, 21, 22) cm

Right Front   Left Front

11 (11½, 11¾, 12¼)"
28 (29, 30, 31) cm

18 (19½, 21¼, 22¾)"
45.5 (49.5, 54, 58) cm

8½ (9¼, 10, 10¾)"
21.5 (23.5, 25.5, 27.5) cm

17"
43 cm

14 (14½, 15¼, 16)"
35.5 (37, 38.5, 40.5) cm

Sleeve

2½ (3¼, 2½, 2½)"
6 (8, 6, 6) cm

10 (10½, 10½, 11¾)"
25.5 (26.5, 26.5, 30) cm

dec 2 (1, 3, 2) st(s) evenly across
row—42 (46, 50, 54) sts rem.
Change to larger needles and work
Blackberry patt until piece measures
3¼" (8 cm), ending after a WS row.
Next row: (RS; dec row) K1, p2tog,
work in patt to last st, k1—1 st
dec'd.
Cont in patt as established and *at
the same time* rep dec row when piece
measures 4¼" (11 cm) and 5½"
(14 cm)—39 (43, 47, 51) sts rem.
   Cont in patt as established until
piece measures 7" (18 cm), ending
after a WS row.
Next row: (RS; inc row) K1, M1,
work in patt to end, k1—1 st inc'd.
Cont in patt as established and *at
the same time* rep inc row when piece
measures 8¾" (22 cm) and 10¼"
(26 cm)—42 (46, 50, 54) sts.
   Cont even in patt until piece
measures 11 (11½, 11¾, 12¼)" (28
[29, 30, 31] cm).

SHAPE ARMHOLE

BO at armhole edge (beg of RS rows) every other row 3 sts 1 (2, 2, 2) time(s), 2 sts 2 (1, 1, 3) time(s), 1 st 3 (4, 4, 2) times—32 (34, 38, 40) sts rem.

Cont in patt until armhole measures 4¼ (4¼, 4¾, 5¼)" (11 [11, 12, 13] cm), ending after a RS row.

SHAPE NECK

BO 5 (5, 6, 7) sts at neck edge (beg of WS rows) once, then 3 sts 1 time, 2 sts 2 times, and 1 st 3 times—17 (19, 22, 23) sts rem. Cont in patt until piece measures 7½ (8, 8¼, 8¾)" (19 [20, 21, 22] cm). BO 5 (6, 7, 7) sts at beg of next RS row, then BO 6 (6, 7, 7) sts at beg of next RS row, then BO 6 (7, 8, 9) sts at beg of next RS row.

RIGHT FRONT

With smaller needles, CO 44 (47, 53, 56) sts.

Row 1: (WS) K2, [p1, k2] to end.
Row 2: K1, p1, k1, [p2, k1] to last 2 sts, p1, k1.

Rep Rows 1 and 2 until ribbing measures 1½" (4 cm), ending after a RS row.

Next row: (WS) Work in patt as established and *at the same time* dec 2 (1, 3, 2) st(s) evenly across row—42 (46, 50, 54) sts rem.

Change to larger needles and work Blackberry patt until piece measures 3¼" (8 cm), ending after a WS row.

Next row: (RS; dec row) K1, work in patt to last 3 sts, p2tog, k1—1 st dec'd.

Cont in patt as established and *at the same time* rep dec row when piece measures 4¼" (11 cm) and 5½" (14 cm)—39 (43, 47, 51) sts rem.

Cont in patt as established until piece measures 7" (18 cm), ending after a WS row.

Next row: (RS; inc row) K1, work in patt to last st, M1, k1—1 st inc'd.

Cont in patt as established and *at the same time* rep inc row when piece measures 8¾" (22 cm) and 10¼" (26 cm)—42 (46, 50, 54) sts.

Cont even in patt until piece measures 11 (11½, 11¾, 12¼)" (28 [29, 30, 31] cm).

SHAPE ARMHOLE

BO at armhole edge (beg of WS rows) every other row 3 sts 1 (2, 2, 2) time(s), 2 sts 2 (1, 1, 3) time(s), 1 st 3 (4, 4, 2) times—32 (34, 38, 40) sts rem.

Cont in patt until armhole measures 4¼ (4¼, 4¾, 5¼)" (11 [11, 12, 13] cm), after a WS row.

SHAPE NECK

BO 5 (5, 6, 7) sts at neck edge (beg of RS rows) once, then 3 sts 1 time, 2 sts 2 times, and 1 st 3 times—17 (19, 22, 23) sts rem.

Cont in patt until piece measures 7½ (8, 8¼, 8¾)" (19 [20, 21, 22] cm). BO 5 (6, 7, 7) sts at beg of next WS row, then BO 6 (6, 7, 7) sts at beg of next WS row, then BO 6 (7, 8, 9) sts at beg of next WS row.

SLEEVES

With smaller needles, CO 50 (53, 53, 59) sts.

Row 1: (WS) K2, [p1, k2] to end.

Row 2: K1, p1, k1, [p2, k1] to last 2 sts, p1, k1.

Rep Rows 1 and 2 until ribbing measures 1½" (4 cm), ending after a RS row.

Next row: (WS) Work in patt as established and *at the same time* inc 0 (inc 1, inc 1, dec 1) st(s) evenly across row—50 (54, 54, 58) sts. Change to larger needles and work Blackberry patt until sleeve measures 2½ (3¼, 2½, 2½)" (6 [8, 6, 6] cm), ending after a WS row.

Next row: (RS; inc row) K1, inc 1, work in patt to last st, inc 1 working new sts into patt, k1—2 sts inc'd.

Cont in patt as established, working new sts into patt and *at the same time* rep inc row every 1½ (1½, 1¼, 1¼)" (4 [4, 3.5, 3.5] cm) 9 (8, 10, 10) more times—70 (72, 76, 80) sts.

Cont in patt until sleeve measures 17" (43 cm) or desired length.

SHAPE SLEEVE CAP

BO 3 sts at beg of next 2 rows, BO 2 (2, 3, 3) sts at beg of next 2 rows, BO 2 sts at beg of next 2 rows, BO 1 st at beg of next 8 (10, 12, 14) rows,

BO 2 sts at beg of next 8 rows, BO 3 sts at beg of next 4 rows, BO 4 sts at beg of next 2 rows, BO rem 12 (12, 12, 14) sts.

FINISHING

With yarn threaded on a tapestry needle, sew shoulder seams.

LEFT FRONT BAND

With larger needles, pick up and knit (see Glossary) 44 (47, 50, 53) sts (about 3 sts for every 4 rows) along left front edge. Work ribbing as foll: K2, [p1, k2] to end. Cont in ribbing patt as established. When ribbing measures 1½" (4 cm), BO sts in patt. Mark button placement with pins: Place one pin about 1" (2.5 cm) from bottom edge and two additional pins evenly spaced between bottom pin and top of band. The fourth button will be placed on neckband. Place corresponding markers (pm) on right front for working buttonholes.

RIGHT FRONT BAND

With larger needles, pick up and knit 44 (47, 50, 53) sts (about 3 sts for every 4 rows) along right front edge. Work in ribbing for ⅜" (1 cm).

Next row: (buttonhole row) Maintaining ribbing patt, work to first marker, *BO 2 sts, work to m, rep from * once more, BO 2 sts, work in ribbing to end. The fourth buttonhole is made on the neckband.

Next row: Work in ribbing patt and CO 2 sts over each buttonhole, maintaining patt.

Cont in ribbing patt until band measures 1¼" (3 cm). BO in ribbing.

NECKBAND

With larger needles and beginning at right front neck edge, pick up and knit 131 (131, 134, 137) sts along neck, ending at left front neck edge. Work ribbing for 1½" (4 cm) and *at the same time*, after ⅝" (1.5 cm), make a buttonhole (BO 2 sts, CO 2 new sts over gap on next row) in neckband aligned with those in right front band. BO in ribbing.

Sew in sleeves. Sew sleeve and side seams. With sewing needle and thread, sew ribbon inside ribbing along right front, around neck and down left front. Sew buttons on left band to correspond with buttonholes. Weave in ends.

lace tiered
SKIRT

A variety of lace patterns, each separated by crocheted picot, gives a lovely structure to this skirt. It is lightweight and wearable, perfect for spring into fall.

FINISHED MEASUREMENTS

30 (32½, 35, 37½)" (76 [82.5, 89, 95] cm) waist circumference; 23½ (23¾, 24, 24½)" (58.5 [60.5, 61, 62] cm) length; 46 (49¾, 52½, 57½)" (116.5 [123.5, 133, 146] cm) wide at bottom edge.

YARN

Sport weight (Fine #2) and crochet thread (Lace #0).
Shown here: Coats Løve Kick (50% cotton, 50% acrylic; 165 yd [150 m]/50 g): #174 sage, 6 (6, 7, 8) balls; Coats Haeklegarn n. 5 (crochet cotton, 100% mercerized cotton, 459 yd [420 m]/100 g): #70 sage, 1 ball. See page 126 for yarn substitution suggestions.

NEEDLES

U.S. size 4 (3.5 mm): 32" (80 cm) circular (cir). Adjust needle sizes if necessary to obtain the correct gauge.

GAUGE:

24 sts and 32 rows = 4" (10 cm) in stockinette stitch and lace.

NOTIONS

Stitch marker (m); tapestry needle; U.S. size B and C (2.25 and 2.5 mm) crochet hook.

stitch guide

CROCHET PICOTS
*Ch 3, 1 sc in first purl st, skip 1
purl st, 1 sl st through next purl
st; rep from * to end of rnd. (See
Glossary for crochet directions.)

SKIRT

With cir needle, CO 276 (299, 322,
345) sts, place marker (pm). Join
for working in the rnd, being careful
not to twist sts. Knit 1 rnd. Work
Rnds 1–12 of Chart A 4 times.

NEXT RND: Knit and dec 3 sts in each
  pattern rep by dec at the purl st in
  center of each pattern as foll: sl 2 sts
  before purl st, k2tog, p2sso—240
  (260, 280, 300) sts rem.

Work 2 more rnds in garter st (knit
1 rnd, purl 1 rnd). Work Rnds 1–16
of Chart B, then work Rnds 1–8
once more. Work garter st for 3 rnds
(knit 1 end, purl 1 rnd, knit 1 rnd).
Work Chart C for ¾" (2 cm). *Note:*
The number of knit sts between
lace motifs changes after dec rnd;
maintain patt so that lace columns
remain aligned.

NEXT RND: *K2tog, work 18 sts in
  patt as established; rep from * to
  end—228 (247, 266, 285) sts rem.

Work even following Chart C as
established for 2" (5 cm).

NEXT RND: *Work 17 sts in patt as
  established, k2tog; rep from * to
  end—216 (234, 252, 270) sts rem.

Work even following Chart C as
established until piece measures 6 (6,
6¼, 6¼)" (15 [15, 16, 16] cm) from
beg of Chart C, ending after Rnd 4.
Work 3 rnds in garter st.

  Work Rnds 1–12 of Chart D for
2½" (6 cm).

NEXT RND: *K2tog, work 16 sts in
  patt as established; rep from * to
  end—204 (221, 238, 255) sts rem.

Work even following Chart D for 1½"
(4 cm). *Note:* The number of knit
sts between lace motifs changes after
dec rnd; maintain patt so that lace
columns remain aligned.

NEXT RND: *Work 15 sts in patt as
  established, k2tog; rep from * to
  end—192 (208, 224, 240) sts rem.

Work even following Chart D as

LACE TIERED SKIRT

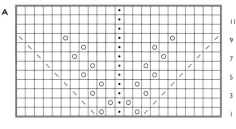

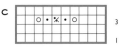

established for 1½" (4 cm).

NEXT RND: *K2tog, work 14 sts in patt as established—180 (195, 210, 225) sts rem.

Work even following Chart D as established until piece measures 6¾ (7, 7, 7½)" (17 [18, 18, 19] cm) from beg of Chart D. BO all sts. Weave in all ends.

CROCHETED EDGINGS

Fold skirt along purl ridge between Charts C and D and hold with top of skirt facing you. Attach crochet thread with 1 sl st through 1 purl st, then work Crochet Picots (see Stitch Guide) to end of rnd. (See Glossary for crochet instructions.) Rep for rem 2 garter ridges. With smaller crochet hook, work picots around bottom edge as foll: [ch 3, 1 sc in next st]. (Try to crochet a little tighter because the picots are close together.) With larger crochet

hook, work 1 rnd sc along the top edge of skirt. With 2 strands of crochet thread held tog and larger crochet hook, make a crochet chain about 50 (52, 55, 57)" (127 [132, 139.5, 144.5] cm). Work cord through gaps in waist edging. Knot ends of cord. Weave in ends.

□	Knit on RS; purl on WS
·	Purl on RS; knit on WS
⊙	Yarnover
⊘	K2tog
⟍	Ssk
⋀	Sl 2 as if to k2tog, k1, p2sso
⊠	P3tog
□	Pattern repeat

⟋⟍ Left twist: K1 tbl in 2nd st on left needle (do not move stitch from left needle), k1 in first st on left needle, slipping both sts from left needle at the same time.

⟍⟋ Right twist: K1 through the front leg of 2nd st on left needle but leave st on left needle, k1 in first st on left needle, slipping both sts off needle at the same time.

diagonal lace
JACKET

The lace panels for the fronts of this jacket are worked diagonally from the raglan edge of the sleeves and the side seam of back, making it not only stylish and shapely but also an intriguing knit.

FINISHED MEASUREMENTS
16½ (17¾, 19, 20, 21¼)" (42 [45, 48, 51 54] cm) back width; 17¾ (19, 20, 21¼, 22½)" (45 [48, 51, 54, 57] cm) back length.

YARN
Worsted weight (Medium #4). *Shown here:* Coats Ombelle (70% mohair, 25% wool, 5% poly-amid; 159 yd [145 m]/50 g): #1010 camel, 5 (5, 6, 7, 7) balls. See page 126 for yarn substitution suggestions.

NEEDLES
U.S. size 10 (6 mm). Adjust needle size if necessary to obtain the correct gauge.

GAUGE
13 sts and 22 rows = 4" (10 cm) in stockinette stitch. 13 sts = 4" (10 cm) in lace pattern.

NOTIONS
Tapestry needle.

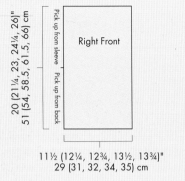

Pick up from sleeve

Pick up from back

20 [21¼, 23, 24¼, 26]"
51 [54, 58.5, 61.5, 66] cm

Right Front

11½ (12¼, 12¾, 13½, 13¾)"
29 (31, 32, 34, 35) cm

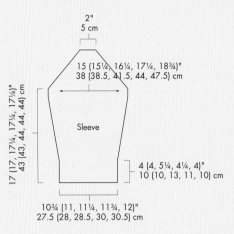

2"
5 cm

15 (15¼, 16¼, 17¼, 18¾)"
38 (38.5, 41.5, 44, 47.5) cm

17 [17, 17¼, 17¼, 17¼]"
43 [43, 44, 44, 44] cm

Sleeve

4 (4, 5¼, 4¼, 4)"
10 (10, 13, 11, 10) cm

10¾ (11, 11¼, 11¾, 12)"
27.5 (28, 28.5, 30, 30.5) cm

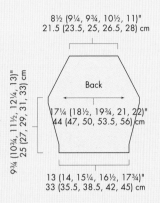

8½ (9¼, 9¾, 10½, 11)"
21.5 (23.5, 25, 26.5, 28) cm

9¾ [10¾, 11½, 12¼, 13]"
25 [27, 29, 31, 33] cm

Back

17¼ (18½, 19¾, 21, 22)"
44 (47, 50, 53.5, 56) cm

13 (14, 15¼, 16½, 17¾)"
33 (35.5, 38.5, 42, 45) cm

SLEEVES

CO 35 (36, 37, 38, 39) sts. Knit 4 rows.

Row 5: (RS) Knit.

Row 6: (WS) K1, purl to last st, k1. Rep Rows 4 and 5, working St st with garter st edges, until piece measures 4 (4, 5¼, 4¼, 4)" (10 [10, 13, 11, 10] cm), ending after a WS row.

Next row: (RS; inc row) K1, M1 (see Glossary), work in St st to last st, M1, k1—2 sts inc'd.

Cont in patt as established and *at the same time* rep inc row every 2 (2, 1½, 1⅜, 1¼)" (5 [5, 4, 3.5, 3] cm) 6 (6, 7, 8, 10) more times—49 (50, 53, 56, 61) sts. Work even in patt until piece measures 17 (17, 17¼, 17¼, 17¼)" (43 [43, 44, 44, 44] cm) or desired length, ending after a WS row.

SHAPE RAGLAN

Next row: (RS; dec row) K2, k2tog, knit to last 4 sts, ssk, k2—2 sts dec'd.

Next row: (WS) K2, purl to last st, k2.

Rep last 2 rows 18 (19, 20, 22, 24) more times—11 (10, 11, 10, 11) sts rem.

Next row: (RS) K2 (1, 2, 1, 2), k2tog 4 times, k1—7 (6, 7, 6, 7) sts rem. BO rem sts.

BACK

CO 42 (46, 50, 54, 58) sts. Knit 4 rows. Work in St st, keeping first st and last st in garter st for edge sts, until piece measures 1½ (2, 2½, 2¾, 3¼)" (4 [5, 6, 7, 8] cm), ending after a WS row.

Next row: (RS; inc row) K1, M1, knit to last st, M1, k1—2 sts inc'd.

Cont in St st maintaining edge sts and *at the same time* rep inc row every 1¼" (3 cm) 6 more times—56 (60, 64, 68, 72) sts.

Cont even in St st, maintaining edge sts, until piece measures 9¾

DIAGONAL JACKET

	Knit on RS; purl on WS
O	Yarnover
/	K2tog
\	Ssk
⋀	Sl 2 tog as if to knit, p2sso
	Pattern repeat

(10¾, 11½, 12¼, 13)" (25 [27, 29, 31, 33] cm), ending after a WS row.

SHAPE RAGLAN

NEXT ROW: (RS; dec row) K2, k2tog, knit to last 4 sts, ssk, k2—2 sts dec'd.

Cont to shape raglan, working dec row every 2nd and 4th row 6 (6, 6, 7, 8) times, then every other row 1 (2, 3, 2, 1) time(s)—28 (30, 32, 34, 34) sts rem. Make sure the back and raglan sleeves match in length for a total of 38 (40, 42, 46, 50) rows. BO all sts.

RIGHT FRONT

Note: Front is worked from side to side.

With yarn threaded on a tapestry needle, sew back raglan edge of right sleeve to right raglan edge of back. Pick up and knit 34 (37, 40, 42, 45) sts along straight right edge of back and 31 (32, 35, 37, 40) sts along raglan edge of right sleeve—65 (69, 75, 79, 85) sts. Purl 1 row. Work Lace chart over center 61 (61, 71, 71, 81) sts with 2 (4, 2, 4, 2) outermost sts at each side always knitted on all rows for 11½ (12¼, 12¾, 13½, 13¾)" (29 [31, 32, 34, 35] cm), ending after Row 8 or Row 16. Knit 4 rows. BO all sts.

LEFT FRONT

Sew back raglan edge of left sleeve to left raglan edge of back. Work as for Right Front.

FINISHING

Sew sleeve seams. Weave in all ends.

frost flowers
JACKET

The lovely lace pattern bordering the front bands of the jacket and continuing up the hood is called "frost flowers." You'll need to concentrate when working the lace because there are pattern rows on both right and wrong sides of the fabric.

FINISHED MEASUREMENTS

33½ (36¼, 39, 42½)" (85 [92, 99, 108] cm) bust circumference; 24¾ (25½, 26½, 27¼)" (63 [65, 67, 69] cm) length.

YARN

DK weight (Light #3).
Shown here: Coats Løve Opera (86% wool, 9% viscose, 5% polyester; 128 yd [117 m]/50 g): #69 petroleum blue, 13 (15, 16, 18) balls. See page 126 for yarn substitution suggestions.

NEEDLES

U.S. size 4 (3.5 mm) and U.S. size 6 (4 mm): straight. U.S. size 4 (3.5 mm): 32" (80 cm) circular (cir). Adjust needle sizes if necessary to obtain the correct gauge.

NOTIONS

Tapestry needle.

GAUGE

21 sts and 29 rows = 4" (10 cm) in stockinette stitch on larger needles.
Lace panel = 6" (15 cm), slightly stretched.

NOTE

Work the first and last stitch of every row in garter stitch (knit on RS and WS).

BACK

With smaller needles, CO 91 (99, 107, 115) sts. Knit 5 rows. With larger needles, work in St st with garter st edges until piece measures 16½ (17, 17¼, 17¾)" (42 [43, 44, 45] cm), ending after a WS row.

SHAPE ARMHOLE

BO 3 sts at beg of next 2 rows, BO 2 sts at beg of next 4 rows, and BO 1 st at beg of next 6 (6, 8, 8) rows—71 (79, 85, 93) sts rem.

Work in St st until armhole measures 8 (8¼, 8¾, 9)" (20 [21, 22, 23] cm), ending after a WS row.

SHAPE SHOULDER

BO 3 (4, 5, 7) sts at beg of next 2 rows, BO 3 (5, 6, 7) sts at beg of next 2 rows, then BO 4 (5, 6, 7) sts at beg of next 2 rows—51 sts rem. Place rem sts on a holder. Note last row of Lace chart worked.

RIGHT FRONT

With smaller needles, CO 68 (72, 76, 80) sts. Knit 5 rows.

NEXT ROW: (RS) With larger needles, work Row 1 of Lace chart over first 36 sts, work in St st to end.

NEXT ROW: (WS) Work in St st to last 36 sts, work Row 2 of Lace chart. Cont in patt as established, working Rows 1–24 of Lace chart over left edge of piece, until piece measures 16½ (17, 17¼, 17¾)" (42 [43, 44, 45] cm), ending after a RS row.

SHAPE ARMHOLE

BO at armhole edge (WS) every

other row as foll: 3 sts once, 2 sts twice, then dec 1 st at armhole edge every row 3 (3, 4, 4) times and *at the same time* beg shaping neck after the first dec row on RS as k2tog after the 36 lace sts. Rep neck dec every 1½" (4 cm) 4 more times. After all decs, 55 (59, 62, 66) sts rem.

Work until armhole measures 8 (8¼, 8¾, 9)" (20 [21, 22, 23] cm), ending after a RS row.

SHAPE SHOULDER

BO at shoulder edge (beg of WS rows) every other row 3 (4, 5, 7) sts, 3 (5, 6, 7) sts, then 4 (5, 6, 7) sts making sure to end on same Lace chart row as back. Place rem 45 sts on a holder.

LEFT FRONT

With smaller needles, CO 68 (72, 76, 80) sts. Knit 5 rows.

NEXT ROW: (RS) With larger needles, work in St st to last 36 sts, work Row 1 of Lace chart over 36 sts.

NEXT ROW: (WS) Work Row 2 of Lace chart on first 36 sts, work in St st to end.

Cont in patt as established, working Rows 1–24 of Lace chart over right edge until piece measures 16½ (17, 17¼, 17¾)" (42 [43, 44, 45] cm), ending after a WS row.

SHAPE ARMHOLE

BO at armhole edge (beg of WS rows) every other row as foll: 3 sts once, 2 sts twice, then dec 1 st at armhole edge every row 3 (3, 4, 4) times and *at the same time* on the first dec, beg

FROST FLOWER LACE

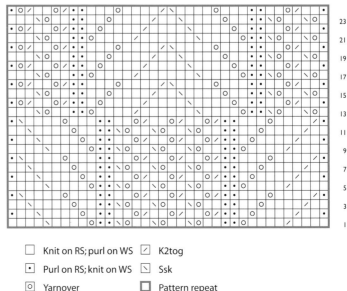

Knit on RS; purl on WS ☑ K2tog

• Purl on RS; knit on WS ☒ Ssk

◉ Yarnover ▢ Pattern repeat

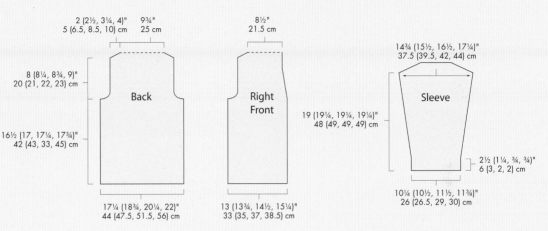

Back

2 (2½, 3¼, 4)"
5 (6.5, 8.5, 10) cm

9¾"
25 cm

8 (8¼, 8¾, 9)"
20 (21, 22, 23) cm

16½ (17, 17¼, 17¾)"
42 (43, 33, 45) cm

17¼ (18¾, 20¼, 22)"
44 (47.5, 51.5, 56) cm

Right Front

8½"
21.5 cm

13 (13¾, 14½, 15¼)"
33 (35, 37, 38.5) cm

Sleeve

14¾ (15½, 16½, 17¼)"
37.5 (39.5, 42, 44) cm

19 (19¼, 19¼, 19¼)"
48 (49, 49, 49) cm

2½ (1¼, ¾, ¾)"
6 (3, 2, 2) cm

10¼ (10½, 11½, 11¾)"
26 (26.5, 29, 30) cm

shaping neck: At front edge (RS), dec with ssk before the 36 lace sts. Rep this dec every 1½" (4 cm) 4 times. After all decs, 55 (59, 62, 66) sts rem.

Work until armhole measures 8 (8¼, 8¾, 9)" (20 [21, 22, 23] cm), ending after a WS row.

SHAPE SHOULDER
BO at shoulder edge (RS) every other row 3 (4, 5, 7) sts, 3 (5, 6, 7) sts, then 4 (5, 6, 7) sts, ending after a WS row on same Lace chart row as back and right front. Place rem 45 sts on a holder.

SLEEVES

With smaller needles, CO 54 (56, 60, 62) sts. Knit 5 rows. With larger needles, work in St st with garter st edges until piece measures 2½ (1¼, ¾, ¾)" (6 [3, 2, 2] cm), ending after a WS row.

NEXT ROW: (RS; inc row) K1, M1 (see Glossary), work in St st to last

st, M1, k1—2 sts inc'd.
Work in St st and *at the same time* rep inc row every 1½" (4 cm) 12 (13, 13, 14) more times—78 (82, 86, 90) sts.

Cont even in patt until piece measures 19 (19¼, 19¼, 19¼)" (48 [49, 49, 49] cm) or desired length.

SHAPE SLEEVE CAP
BO 3 sts at beg of the next 16 (18, 18, 20) rows. BO rem 30 (28, 32, 30) sts.

FINISHING

HOOD
With yarn threaded on a tapestry needle, sew shoulder seams. Sew in sleeves, then sew underarm and side seams. Replace 141 held sts (45 left front sts, 51 back sts, 45 right front sts) on larger needles and rejoin yarn.

NEXT ROW: (RS) Beg with next row of chart, work Lace chart over first 36 sts, work in St st to last 36 sts, work Lace chart over 36 sts.

Cont in patt until hood measures 11¾ (11¾, 12¼, 12¼)" (30 [30, 31, 31] cm) at center back. Place 68 sts on one needle and 69 sts on other needle. With three-needle method (see Glossary) and RS held tog, join sides of hood. BO rem (center) st.

EDGINGS
With cir, pick up and knit (see Glossary) about 398 (405, 424, 430) sts (3 sts for every 4 rows) along front edges, including hood. Knit 5 rows. BO all sts.

BELT
With larger needles, CO 8 sts. Work in garter st until piece measures 47¼ to 55¼" (120 to 140 cm). BO all sts.

BELT LOOPS
With larger needles, CO 10 sts. Knit 4 rows. BO all sts. Sew a loop to each side at waist, placing top of loop about 7 (7½, 7¾, 8)" (18 [19, 19.5, 20.5] cm) below armhole or at desired waist position.

MOHAIR-EDGED
sweater

The heavy wool yarn makes a lovely contrast against the fine mohair in this otherwise plain sweater. The collar can be folded as a shawl collar or worn flat as shown here.

FINISHED MEASUREMENTS
35½ (38¼, 40½, 43¼)" (90 [97, 103, 110] cm) bust circumference; 22¾ (23¾, 24½, 25¼)" (58 [60, 62, 64] cm) long.

YARN
Chunky (Bulky #5) and worsted (Medium #4).

Shown here: Coats Løve Cosy (100% superwash wool; 137 yd [125 m]/100 g): #30 natural, 4 (5, 5, 6) balls (wool); and Coats Fonty Ombelle (70% mohair, 25% wool, 5% polyamid; 159 yd [145 m]/50 g): #1008 natural, 2 balls (mohair). See page 126 for yarn substitution suggestions.

NEEDLES
U.S. size 8 (5 mm) and U.S. size 10¾ (7 mm): straight. U.S. size 8 (5 mm): 32" (80 cm) circular (cir). U.S. size H (5 mm): crochet hook. Adjust needle sizes if necessary to obtain the correct gauge.

NOTIONS
Tapestry needle; one ½" (1.3 cm) button.

GAUGE
12 sts and 18 rows = 4" (10 cm) in stockinette on larger needles with wool.

NOTE
Work the first and last stitch of every row in garter stitch (knit on RS and WS).

BACK

With smaller needles and mohair, CO 67 (73, 79, 85) sts.

Row 1: (WS) K1, p1, k3, [p3, k3] to last 2 sts, p1, k1.

Work in ribbing as established (working sts as they appear) for 4 more rows and *at the same time* work the first and last sts of each row in garter st.

With larger needles and wool, knit 1 row and *at the same time* dec 11 (13, 15, 17) sts as p2tog evenly across row—56 (60, 64, 68) sts rem.

Cont in St st with garter st edges until piece measures 4" (10 cm), ending after a WS row.

Next row: (RS; dec row) K1, ssk, knit to last 3 sts, k1tog, k1—2 sts dec'd.

Cont in St st with garter st edges and *at the same time* rep dec row when piece measures 6¾" and 9½" (17 and 24 cm)—50 (54, 58, 62) sts rem.

Cont even in St st until piece measures 12¼ (12¾, 13, 13½)" (31 [32, 33, 34] cm), ending after a WS row.

*Next row: (RS; inc row) K1, M1 (see Glossary), knit to last st, M1, k1—2 sts inc'd.

Work 5 rows even in patt.

Rep from * once, then rep inc row once more—56 (60, 64, 68) sts.

Cont in patt until piece measures 15½ (15¾, 16¼, 16½)" (39 [40, 41, 42] cm) from CO, ending after a WS row.

SHAPE ARMHOLES

BO 2 (2, 2, 3) sts at beg of next 2 rows, BO 2 sts at beg of next 2 (2, 2, 4) rows, then BO 1 st at beg of next 6 (8, 8, 4) rows—42 (44, 48, 50) sts rem.

Cont in patt until armhole measures 7 (7½, 8, 8¼)" (18 [19, 20, 21] cm), ending after a WS row.

SHAPE NECK AND SHOULDERS

Next row: (RS) K10 (11, 12, 13), place the center 22 (22, 24, 24) sts on a holder for neck, join another ball and k10 (11, 12, 13). Work each side separately and *at the same time* shape shoulder by binding off on armhole edge 5 (5, 6, 6) sts, then 5 (6, 6, 7) sts.

FRONT

Work as for back until front measures 13½ (14¼, 15, 15¾)" (34 [36, 38, 40] cm), shaping side seams as for back and ending after a WS row—56 (60, 64, 68) sts.

SHAPE ARMHOLES AND NECK

Next row: K23 (25, 27, 29), join another ball of yarn and BO center 10 sts, knit to end.

Work each side separately.

RIGHT SIDE

Row 1: (WS) K1, purl to last st, k1.

Row 2: (RS; dec row) K1, k2tog,

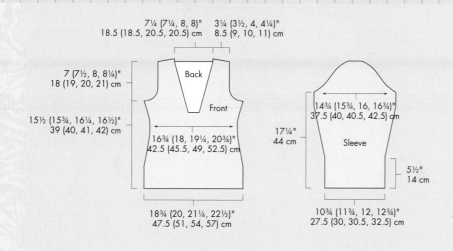

7¼ (7¼, 8, 8)"
18.5 (18.5, 20.5, 20.5) cm

3¼ (3½, 4, 4¼)"
8.5 (9, 10, 11) cm

7 (7½, 8, 8¼)"
18 (19, 20, 21) cm

Back

Front

15½ (15¾, 16¼, 16½)"
39 (40, 41, 42) cm

16¾ (18, 19¼, 20¾)"
42.5 (45.5, 49, 52.5) cm

14¾ (15¾, 16, 16¾)"
37.5 (40, 40.5, 42.5) cm

17¼"
44 cm

Sleeve

5½"
14 cm

18¾ (20, 21¼, 22½)"
47.5 (51, 54, 57) cm

10¾ (11¾, 12, 12¾)"
27.5 (30, 30.5, 32.5) cm

knit to end—1 st dec'd.
Cont in St st and rep neck dec row every 8th row 5 (5, 6, 6) more times and *at the same time* when piece measures 15½ (15¾, 16¼, 16½)" (39 [40, 41, 42] cm) from CO, BO at armhole edge every other row: 2 (2, 2, 3) sts once, 2 sts 1 (1, 1, 2) time(s), then dec 1 st at every row 3 (4, 4, 2) times—10 (11, 12, 13) sts rem after neck and shoulder decs.

Work in St st over rem sts until piece is same length as back and shape shoulder by binding off from armhole edge 5 (5, 6, 6) sts, then 5 (6, 6, 7) sts.

LEFT SIDE
Rejoin yarn.
Row 1: (WS) K1, purl to last st, k1.
Row 2: (RS; dec row) Knit to last 3 sts, ssk, k1—1 st dec'd.
Cont in St st and rep neck dec row every 8th row 5 (5, 6, 6) more times

and *at the same time* when piece measures 15½ (15¾, 16¼, 16½)" (39 [40, 41, 42] cm), BO at armhole edge every other row: 2 (2, 2, 3) sts once, 2 sts 1 (1, 1, 2) time(s), then dec 1 st at armhole edge every row 3 (4, 4, 2) times—10 (11, 12, 13) sts rem after neck and shoulder decs.

Work in St st over rem sts until piece is same length as back. Shape shoulder by BO 5 (5, 6, 6) sts, then 5 (6, 6, 7) sts from armhole edge.

SLEEVES
With smaller needles and mohair, CO 43 (43, 49, 49) sts. Work ribbing as for back until piece measures 5½" (14 cm), ending after a WS row.
Next row: (RS; dec row) With larger needles and wool, work in St st with garter st edges and *at the same time* dec 11 (8, 13, 11) sts as

p2tog evenly spaced across—32 (35, 36, 38) sts rem.
Work in St st, keeping edge sts in garter st for 7 rows.
*Next row: (RS; inc row) K1, M1, knit to last st, M1, k1—2 sts inc'd.
Work 7 rows even.
Rep from * 5 more times—44 (47, 48, 50) sts.

Cont in patt until piece measures 17¼" (44 cm) or desired length to sleeve cap.

SHAPE SLEEVE CAP
BO 2 (2, 2, 3) sts at beg of next 2 rows, BO 2 sts at beg of next 2 rows, BO 2 (2, 1, 2) st(s) at beg of next 2 rows, BO 1 st at beg of next 12 (12, 12, 10) rows, BO 2 sts at beg of next 2 rows, BO 2 (2, 2, 3) sts at beg of next 2 rows, BO 3 (4, 5, 4) sts at beg of next 2 rows, BO rem 6 (7, 8, 8) sts.

FINISHING AND COLLAR

With yarn threaded on a tapestry needle, sew shoulder seams. With cir and mohair and beg at BO of center neck sts, pick up and knit (see Glossary) 15 sts for every 4" (10 cm) for 42 (42, 45, 48) sts along each front edge (or about 3 sts for every 4 rows). At center back, pick up sts in same manner and *at the same time* inc 1 st in about every 4th st until there are about 35 sts along back neck—about 119 (119, 125, 131) sts total. Make sure the stitch count is a multiple of 6 + 5.

ROW 1: (WS) K1, [p3, k3] across to
    last 4 sts, p3, k1.

Work in patt, keeping edge sts in garter st, for 2 rows. Cut yarn and attach it just before the center 33 sts on back. Work 2 rows over these sts.

SHORT-ROWS: Continue in ribbing but work 3 more sts in ribbing at the end of each row so that the ribbing is gradually worked over more and more sts (short-rows). At the end of every row (before working the 3 new rib sts), M1, then work the 3 new sts. Turn and work back but work the M1 st tog with the st before it (the last of the 3 new sts) to avoid a hole. Work 3 more sts 9 (10, 10, 11) times at each side. Continue in ribbing over all sts until ribbing is same width at the ends as BO sts at center front. BO in ribbing.

Sew the sides of the collar at the base of the front, with the right side overlapping the left. *Note:* The shawl collar should be about 4" (10 cm) wide at its base at center front and about 9¾" (25 cm) wide at center back.

Sew in sleeves and sew underarm and side seams. Lightly steam the collar edge on WS to prevent rolling.

CROCHETED FLOWER

Wrap mohair around one finger 3 or 4 times. Carefully remove ring and hold it together with 1 sl st around the ring. (See Glossary for crochet instructions.)

RND 1: Ch 1, sc 17 in ring. End with 1 sl st in first ch.

RND 2: Ch 6, skip 2 sc, 1 sc in next sc, *ch 4, skip 2 sc, 1 sc in next sc; rep from * 3 more times, end with ch 4, 1 sl st in the 2nd of the first 6 ch.

RND 3: Ch 1, work (1 sc, 1 hdc, 3 dc, 1 hdc, 1 sc) in every ch-4 loop, end with 1 sl st in first sc.

RND 4: Work 1 sl st in back of first sc of 2nd rnd, *ch 5, hold yarn behind work and work 1 sl st in back around the next sc of 2nd rnd; rep from * 4 more times, ch 5, 1 sl st in same sc as first sl st.

RND 5: Work (1 sc, 1 hdc, 5 dc, 1 hdc, 1 sc) around every ch-5 loop, end rnd with 1 sl st in first sc. Fasten off.

Pull CO tail to draw in center of flower. Sew button to center of flower. Sew or pin flower to sweater.

shawl collar
JACKET

The classic lines of this jacket are dressed up with a dramatic rib-and-bobble pattern. The texture continues with a seed-stitch shawl collar and strong vertical lines created by twisted ribs on the sleeves and back.

FINISHED MEASUREMENTS

36¾ (39½, 42¼, 45)" (93 [100, 107, 114] cm) bust circumference; 22¾ (23¾, 24½, 25¼)" (58 [60, 62, 64] cm) long.

YARN

Worsted weight (Medium #4). *Shown here:* Coats Løve Ragsokgarn (70% superwash wool, 30% nylon; 88 yd [80 m]/50 g): #30 natural, 13 (14, 16, 17) balls. See page 126 for yarn substitution suggestions.

NEEDLES

U.S. size (4.5 mm) and U.S. size 9 (5.5 mm). Adjust needle sizes if necessary to obtain the correct gauge.

NOTIONS

Tapesty needle; sewing needle and thread; six ¾" (2 cm) buttons.

GAUGE

16 sts and 22 rows = 4" (10 cm) in stockinette on larger needles.

NOTE

Work the first and last stitch of every row in garter stitch (knit on RS and WS).

stitch guide

SEED STITCH
Row 1: [K1, p1] to last st, k1.
Row 2 and all following rows:
Work sts opposite of how they
appear (i.e., knit the purl sts
and purl the knit sts).

BACK

With smaller needles, CO 79 (85,
89, 95) sts. Keeping first and last
st of each row in garter st, work in
seed st for 5 rows. Change to larger
needles.
Row 1: (RS) K1 (edge st), p3 (6, 8,
1), *k1 tbl, p9; rep from * to last 5
(8, 10, 3) sts, k1 tbl, p3 (6, 8, 1),
k1 (edge st).
Row 2: (WS) K1 (edge st), k3 (6, 8,
1), *p1, k9; rep from * to last 5 (8,
10, 3) sts, p1, k3 (6, 8, 1), k1 (edge
st).
Next row: (RS; dec row) K1, ssk,
work in patt to last 3 sts, k2tog,
k1—2 sts dec'd.
Cont in patt, working dec sts into
patt and *at the same time* rep dec row
when piece measures 4¼" (11 cm),
5½" (14 cm), and 6¾" (17 cm)—71
(77, 81, 87) sts.
Cont in patt until piece measures
8¾ (9, 9½, 9¾)" (22 [23, 24,
25] cm), ending after a WS row.

Next row: (RS; inc row) K1, M1
(see Glossary), work in patt to last
st, M1, k1—2 sts inc'd.
Cont in patt, working inc sts into
patt and *at the same time* rep inc row
every 1¼" (3 cm) 3 more times—79
(85, 89, 95) sts.
Cont in patt until piece measures
14¼ (14½, 15, 15½)" (36 [37, 38,
39] cm), ending after a WS row.

SHAPE ARMHOLES AND
NECK
BO 3 sts at beg of next 2 rows, BO
2 sts at beg of next 2 (4, 4, 6) rows,
then BO 1 st at beg of next 6 (4, 6,
6) rows—63 (67, 69, 71) sts rem.
Cont in patt until piece measures
7½ (8, 8¼, 8¾)" (19 [20, 21,
22] cm), ending after a WS row.
Next row: Work 21 (23, 24, 25)
sts in patt, join another strand of
yarn and BO center 21 sts, work
in patt to end.
Working each side separately, BO 1
st on next row at neck edge—20 (22,
23, 24) sts rem.
When armhole measures 8¼ (8¾,
9, 9¼)" (21 [22, 23, 24] cm), shape
shoulder by binding off at each
shoulder edge every other row 6 (7,
7, 8) sts once, 7 (7, 8, 8) sts once, 7
(8, 8, 8) sts once. Rejoin yarn and
work other side the same way.

LEFT FRONT

With smaller needles, CO 44 (47,
49, 52) sts. Work 5 rows in seed st

with garter st edges.
Next row: With larger needles, k1
(edge st), work Bobble over next
38 (41, 43, 46) sts as indicated
for size, work 5 sts in seed st for
front band.
Cont in patt as established until
piece measures 3¼" (8 cm), ending
after a WS row.
Next row: (RS; dec row) K1, ssk,
work in patt to last st, k1—1 st
dec'd.
Cont in patt, working dec sts into
patt and *at the same time* rep dec row
when piece measures 4¼" (11 cm),
5½" (14 cm), and 6¾" (17 cm)—40
(43, 45, 48) sts rem.
Cont in patt until piece measures
8¾ (9, 9½, 9¾)" (22 [23, 24,
25] cm), ending after a WS row.
Next row: (RS; inc row) K1, M1,
work in patt to last st, k1—1 st
inc'd.
Cont in patt, working inc sts into
patt and *at the same time* rep inc row
every 1¼" (3 cm) 3 more times—44
(47, 49, 52) sts.
Cont in patt until piece measures
14¼ (14½, 15, 15½)" (36 [37, 38,
39] cm), ending after a WS row.

SHAPE ARMHOLE
AND COLLAR
BO 3 sts at beg of next RS row.
Note: Read the following directions before working further, as
several actions are performed at the
same time.

BO 2 sts at beg of next RS row 1 (2, 2, 3) time(s), then dec 1 st at armhole edge every row 3 (1, 3, 3) time(s) and *at the same time* beg collar ⅜" (1 cm) after beg of armhole: on RS, work until 2 sts rem, M1, work 1 st in patt, M1, work last st in patt.

NEXT ROW: (short-row) Work seed st over first 7 sts, turn, work seed st over 7 sts.

Work seed st over outermost 7 sts and in patt over rem sts. Working new sts in seed st and working incs 1 st in from front edge, inc 1 st on every row for collar 8 times, then inc 1 st every other row 7 (7, 6, 6) times, then 1 st 2 (2, 3, 3) times every 4th row (24 collar sts after incs are completed) and *at the same time* when armhole measures 2"

(5 cm), begin neck shaping on next RS row: work to 2 sts before collar sts, dec 1 (as k2tog or p2tog following patt), work collar sts in seed st. Work dec row every other row 8 times, then every 4th row until 44 (46, 47, 48) sts rem.

Work until armhole measures 8¼ (8¾, 9, 9¼)" (21 [22, 23, 24] cm), then shape shoulder by binding off at shoulder edge every other row: 6 (7, 7, 8) sts, 7 (7, 8, 8) sts, 7 (8, 8, 8) sts—24 collar sts rem.

SHORT-ROWS: Continue in seed st: *Work 2 rows over all sts, work 2 rows over outermost 16 sts at front edge only.

Rep from * until collar measures about 3" (7.5 cm) at inner edge (measure along back neck as collar

must reach center back). Place sts on a holder.

RIGHT FRONT

Work as for left front, reversing all shaping, until piece measures ⅜ (⅜, ¾, ¾)" (1 [1, 2, 2] cm), ending after a WS row.

NEXT ROW: (RS; buttonhole row 1) Work 2 sts in seed st, BO 2 sts, work in patt to end.

NEXT ROW: (WS; buttonhole row 2) Work in patt to BO sts, use the cable method (see Glossary) to CO 2 sts over gap, work in patt to end.

Work in patt as established and rep 2 buttonhole rows when piece measures 3½ (3½, 4, 4)" (9 [9, 10, 10] cm), 6¾ (6¾, 7, 7)" (17 [17,

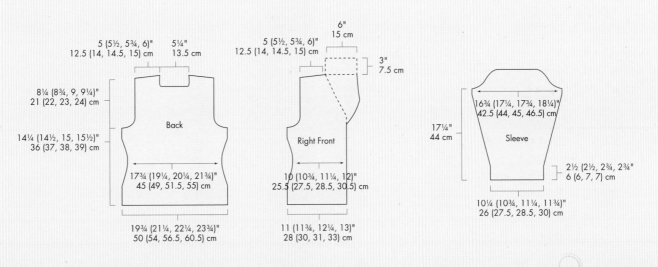

BOBBLE

RIGHT FRONT

LEFT FRONT

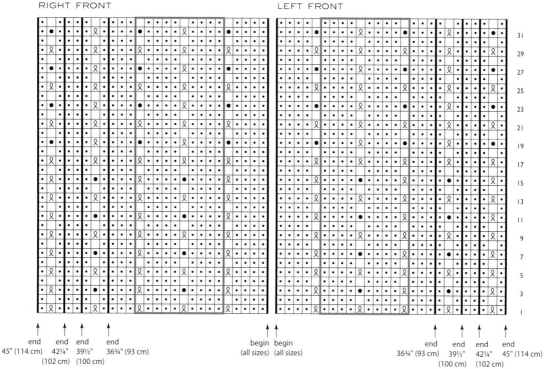

end 45" (114 cm)
end 42¼" (102 cm)
end 39½" (100 cm)
end 36¾" (93 cm)

begin (all sizes)
begin (all sizes)

end 36¾" (93 cm)
end 39½" (100 cm)
end 42¼" (102 cm)
end 45" (114 cm)

□ Knit on RS; purl on WS

· Purl on RS; knit on WS

● Bobble: (K1, yo, k1) into the same st (3 sts),
turn, [k1f&b] in next 3 sts (6 sts), sl 5 sts
individually over first st—1 st rem.

Ω K1tbl on RS, p1tbl on WS

□ Pattern repeat

18, 18] cm), 9¾ (9¾, 10¼, 10¼)"
(25 [25, 26, 26] cm), 13 (13, 13½,
13½)" (33 [33, 34.5, 34.5] cm),
and 15¾ (16¼, 16½, 17)" (40 [41,
42, 43] cm).

Cont in patt as for Left Front,
reversing shaping. (For neck shaping, work as foll on RS row: Work
collar sts in seed st, ssk, work to end
of row.)

SLEEVES

With smaller needles, CO 41 (43,
45, 47) sts. Work 5 rows in seed st.
Row 1: (RS) With larger needles, k1,
p9 (0, 1, 2), [k1 tbl, p9] to last 11
(2, 3, 4) sts, k1 tbl, p9 (0, 1, 2),
k1.
Row 2: (WS) K1 (edge st), k9 (0, 1,
2), [p1, k9] across, end with p1,
k9 (0, 1, 2), k1 (edge st).
Cont in patt as established, keeping
first and last sts of every row in
garter st, until piece measures 2½,
2½, 2¾, 2¾)" (6 [6, 7, 7] cm),
ending after a WS row.
*Next row: (RS; inc row) K1, M1,
work in patt to last st, M1, k1—2
sts inc'd.
Cont in patt as established, working
inc sts into patt, for 5 rows.
Rep from * 12 more times—67
(69, 71, 73) sts.

Cont in patt until piece measures
17¼" (44 cm) or desired length to
sleeve cap.

SHAPE SLEEVE CAP
BO 3 sts at beg of next 4 (4, 2, 2)
rows, BO 2 sts at beg of next 4 (4,
6, 6) rows, BO 1 st at beg of next 4
(4, 6, 8) rows, BO 2 sts at beg of
the next 4 (6, 8, 8) rows, BO 4 sts
at beg of next 2 rows, BO rem 27
(25, 23, 23) sts.

FINISHING

With yarn threaded on a tapestry
needle, sew shoulder seams. Use
three-needle method (see Glossary)
and yarn to join collar at center
back neck. Sew down collar along
back neck (using a ½ st seam so that
the seamline won't be too thick).
Sew in sleeves, then sew side and
underarm seams. With sewing
needle and thread, sew buttons to
right front band to correspond with
buttonholes. Weave in all ends.

lace SCARF

This elegant little scarf is a study in contrasts: a knitted panel in soft, plush mohair is surrounded by a crocheted lace edging in a smooth, light linen blend. The resulting sweet confection is the perfect gift—if you can bear to part with it.

FINISHED MEASUREMENTS

About 7" (18 cm) wide and 34¾" (88 cm) long.

YARN

DK weight (Light #3).
Shown here: Coats Fonty Kidopale (70% kid mohair, 30% polyamide; 275 yd [250 m]/25 g): powder 300, 1 ball (mohair), and Coats HP Løve Lima (38% linen, 31% cotton; 31% viscose; 223 yd [104 m]/50 g): powder 211, 1 ball (linen). See page 126 for yarn substitution suggestions.

NEEDLES

U.S. size 6 (4 mm). U.S. size D (3 mm) crochet hook. Adjust needle size if necessary to obtain the correct gauge.

GAUGE

18½ sts and 25 rows = 4" (10 cm) in lace pattern with mohair.

SCARF

With mohair, CO 27 sts loosely. Purl 1 row. Work Lace chart until scarf measures 31½" (80 cm) or desired length, ending as indicated. BO loosely. Weave in ends.

EDGINGS

With crochet hook and linen and beg on BO row, work 1 row sc around the entire scarf, working about 20 sc for every 4" (10 cm) along the long sides and 34 sc along CO and BO edges. (See Glossary for crochet instructions.) Do not cut yarn; continue with lace edging along the first short end.

Row 1: Work 1 row of sc. Ch 1, turn.

Row 2: 1 sc in each of the first 3 sc, *ch 9, skip 3 sc, 1 sc in each of the next 5 sc. Rep from * 4 times total, however on the last rep, work only 1 sc in each of the last 3 sc. Ch 1, turn.

Row 3: 1 sc in each of the first 2 sc, *ch 5, 1 sc around the ch-9 loop, ch 5, skip 1 sc, 1 sc in each of the next 3 sc. Rep from * a total of 4 times, however on last rep, work only 1 sc in each of the last 2 sc. Ch 1, turn.

Row 4: 1 sc in first sc, *ch 5, skip 1 sc, 1 sc in next sc. Rep from * across. Ch 1, turn.

Row 5: 1 sc in first sc, *ch 5, make a triple double loop in the next st (1 sl st in next sc, [ch 7, 1 sl st] 3 times in the same sc as for first sl st), ch 5, 1 sc in next sc. Rep from * 4 times total. Do not turn but continue with sc along one long side of the scarf (1 sc for each row along the lace edging), then work lace edging on other short edge of scarf. Finish with sc along the other long side of scarf. Fasten off and weave in tails on WS.

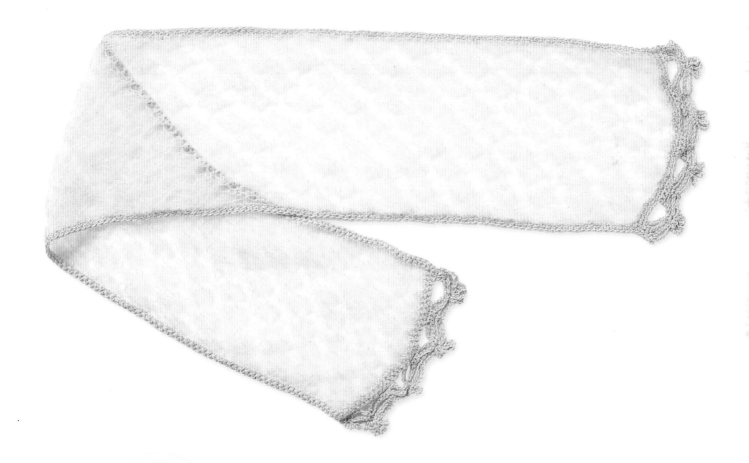

LACE

Chart legend:

- ☐ Knit on RS; purl on WS
- · Purl on RS; knit on WS
- ○ Yarnover
- ╱ K2tog
- ╲ Ssk
- ⋋ Sssk
- ☐ Pattern repeat

lace scarf
109

rib knit
VEST

You can wear this piece as a vest or as a warm shell on a cold day. The ribbed vest hugs the figure, but the sizes are very flexible. The lace pattern on the front is a lovely feminine detail.

FINISHED MEASUREMENTS

27½ (30¼, 33, 35½, 38¼)" (70 [77, 84, 90, 97 cm]) bust circumference; 20½ (21¼, 22, 22¾, 23¾)" (52 [54, 56, 58, 60] cm) long. *Note:* Finished garment will stretch significantly; check gauge carefully and choose a size with little ease, if any.

YARN

DK weight (Light #3).
Shown here: Sandnes Alpakka (100% baby alpaca; 120 yd [110 m]/50 g): #9655 army, 4 (4, 5, 5, 5) balls. See page 126 for yarn substitution suggestions.

NEEDLES

U.S. size 6 (4 mm). Adjust needle size if necessary to obtain the correct gauge.

NOTIONS

Stitch markers (m); tapestry needle.

GAUGE

23 sts = 4" (10 cm) in ribbing, slightly stretched.

NOTE

Work the first and last stitch of every row in garter stitch (knit on RS and WS) except where indicated.

BACK

CO 82 (90, 98, 106, 114) sts.

Row 1: (WS) K1 (edge st), k1, p2, [k2, p2] to last 2 sts, k1, k1 (edge st).

Work ribbing patt as established, keeping first and last sts of every row in garter st, until piece measures 13 (13½, 13¾, 14¼, 14½)" (33 [34, 35, 36, 37] cm), ending after a WS row.

SHAPE ARMHOLES

BO 2 sts at beg of next 2 rows—78 (86, 94, 102, 110) sts rem.

Row 1: (RS) Sl 1 pwise with yarn in back (wyb), k1, p2, p3tog, p1, [k2, p2] to last 10 sts, k2, p1, k3tog tbl, p2, k2—4 sts dec'd.

Row 2: Sl 1 with yarn in front (wyf), work in patt to end.

Row 3: Sl 1, k1, p2, k3tog, k1, [p2, k2] to last 8 sts, k1, k3tog tbl, p2, k2—4 sts dec'd.

Row 4: Rep Row 2.

Rep Rows 1–4 one (two, two, two,

three) more times—62 (62, 70, 78, 78) sts rem.

Cont in [p2, k2] patt, slipping first st of every row either as a knit or purl to maintain patt, until armhole measures 6 (6¼, 6¾, 7, 7½)" (15 [16, 17, 18, 19] cm).

Next row: K14 (14, 18, 22, 22), join a new ball of yarn and BO 34 sts for neck, k14 (14, 18, 22, 22). Working each side separately and sl the outermost st at neck edge as for armhole edge, work until armhole measures 7½ (8, 8¼, 8¾, 9)" (19 [20, 21, 22, 23] cm), then place rem 14 (14, 18, 22, 22) sts on a holder for shoulder.

FRONT

Work as for back until piece measures 10¼ (10¾, 11½, 11¾, 12¼)" (26 [27, 29, 30, 31] cm), ending after a WS row.

Next row: (RS) Work 22 (26,

30, 34, 38) sts in ribbing, place marker (pm), work Lace patt over 38 sts, pm, work in ribbing to end.

Cont in patt as established. *Note:* After Row 1 of Lace patt, the number of sts between m is reduced to 33 (due to decs on Row 1)—77 (85, 93, 101, 109) sts rem.

SHAPE ARMHOLES

Cont in patt, working Lace chart over center sts and *at the same time* when piece measures 13 (13½, 13¾, 14¼, 14½)" (33 [34, 35, 36, 37] cm), shape armholes as for back: BO 2 sts at armhole edge once, then rep Rows 1–4 two (three, three, three, four) times, working Lace chart over center sts—57 (57, 65, 73, 73) sts rem. Work in patt as established until armhole measures 2¾" (7 cm). Work 19 (19, 23, 27, 27) sts, join another ball of yarn and BO center 19 sts, work in patt to end.

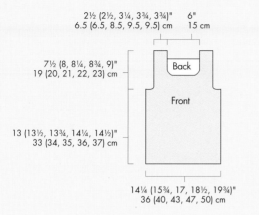

2½ (2½, 3¼, 3¾, 3¾)"   6"
6.5 (6.5, 8.5, 9.5, 9.5) cm   15 cm

7½ (8, 8¼, 8¾, 9)"
19 (20, 21, 22, 23) cm

Back

Front

13 (13½, 13¾, 14¼, 14½)"
33 (34, 35, 36, 37) cm

14¼ (15¾, 17, 18½, 19¾)"
36 (40, 43, 47, 50) cm

Working each side separately, BO 2 sts at neck edge once, then 1 st at neck edge 3 times—14 (14, 18, 22, 22) sts. Work until armhole measures 7½ (8, 8¼, 8¾, 9)" (19 [20, 21, 22, 23] cm), then place rem 14 (14, 18, 22, 22) sts on a holder for shoulder.

FINISHING

Replace held sts for back shoulders on needles. Use the three-needle method (see Glossary) to join front and back shoulders. With yarn threaded on a tapestry needle, sew side seams.

LACE

3

1

set-up 1

☐ Knit on RS; purl on WS

• Purl on RS; knit on WS

○ Yarnover

✓ K2tog

✺ Ssk

☐ Pattern repeat

lapel JACKET

This classic blazer-style jacket gets its rich texture from a simple broken rib pattern. Thoughtful finishes such as a crocheted edging and turned-back lapels make this an everyday favorite.

FINISHED MEASUREMENTS

35½ (37½, 40¼, 42½)" (90 [95, 102, 108] cm) bust circumference; 24 (24¾, 25½, 26½)" (61 [63, 65, 67] cm) long.

YARN

Worsted weight (Medium #4). *Shown here:* Coats Løve Lino (63% cotton, 37% linen; 76 yd [70 m]/50 g): #58 blue, 13 (14, 15, 17) balls. See page 126 for yarn substitution suggestions.

NEEDLES

U.S. size 9 (5.5 mm). U.S. size F (4 mm) crochet hook. Adjust needle size if necessary to obtain the correct gauge.

NOTIONS

Tapestry needle; sewing needle and thread; three ¾" buttons.

GAUGE

16 sts and 24 rows = 4" (10 cm) in pattern stitch.

BACK

CO 74 (78, 84, 88) sts.

Row 1: (RS) K1 (edge st), work Jacket chart to last st, k1 (edge st).

Cont in patt as established, working first and last sts of every row in garter st, until piece measures 1½ (1½, 2, 2)" (4 [4, 5, 5] cm), ending after a WS row.

Next row: (RS; dec row) K1, ssk, work in patt to last 3 sts, k2tog, k1—2 sts dec'd.

Cont in patt working dec sts into patt, and *at the same time* rep dec row every 1½" (4 cm) 3 more times total—66 (70, 76, 80) sts rem.

Cont in patt until piece measures 8¼ (8¾, 9, 9½)" (21 [22, 23, 24] cm), ending after a WS row.

Next row: (RS; inc row) K1, M1 (see Glossary), work in patt to last st, M1, k1—2 sts inc'd.

Cont in patt, working inc sts into patt and *at the same time* rep inc row every 1½" (4 cm) three more times—74 (78, 84, 88) sts.

Cont in patt until piece measures 16¼ (16½, 17, 17¼)" (41 [42, 43, 44] cm).

SHAPE ARMHOLES

BO 3 sts at beg of next 2 (2, 2, 4) rows, BO 2 sts at beg of next 2 (2, 4, 2) rows, then BO 1 st at beg of next 6 (8, 6, 6) rows—58 (60, 64, 66) sts rem.

Cont even in patt until armhole measures 7½ (8, 8¼, 8¾)" (19

[20, 21, 22] cm).

Next row: Work 17 (18, 19, 20) sts in patt, join a new ball of yarn and BO 24 (24, 26, 26) sts for neck, work in patt to end.

Working each side separately, BO 1 st at neck edge on next row and *at the same time* BO at shoulder edge every other row 5 (5, 6, 6) sts, 5 (6, 6, 6) sts, then 6 (6, 6, 7) sts.

LEFT FRONT

CO 36 (38, 41, 43) sts.

Row 1: (RS) K1 (edge st), work Jacket chart to last st, k1 (edge st).

Note: Read the rest of this section before knitting further, as several procedures are worked simultaneously.

Cont in patt, inc 1 st as M1 at front edge every other row 2 times, then every 4 rows 2 times and *at the same time* shape side decs as foll:

Next row: (RS; dec row) K1, ssk, work in patt to last st, k1—1 st dec'd.

Cont in patt, working dec sts into patt and *at the same time* rep dec row every 1½" (4 cm) 3 more times.

Cont in patt until piece measures 8¼ (8¾, 9, 9½)" (21 [22, 23, 24] cm), ending after a WS row—36 (38, 41, 43) sts.

Next row: (RS; inc row) K1, M1, work in patt to last st, k1—1 st inc'd.

Cont in patt, working inc sts into patt, and *at the same time* rep inc row every 1½" (4 cm) three more times and *at the same time* begin shaping as for lapel as M1 two

sts from edge when front measures 11½ (11¾, 12¼, 12¾)" (29 [30, 31, 32] cm). (*Note:* Because the lapel folds back against RS of jacket, patt for lapel is the reverse of jacket body. On 4th and 8th patt rows, work in rev St st.)

Inc 1 st between lapel sts and jacket front every 8 rows 6 times, working new sts in patt as for the first two lapel sts and *at the same time* when same length as back to underarm, shape armhole as for back: BO at armhole edge every other row 3 sts 1 (1, 1, 2) time(s), 2 sts 1 (1, 2, 1) time(s), dec 1 st at armhole edge every row 3 (4, 3, 3) times—39 (40, 42, 43) sts rem.

SHAPE NECK

Cont in patt until armhole measures 5½ (5½, 5½, 6)" (13 [14, 14, 15] cm).

At front lapel, BO 9 sts once, then 5 sts once, 3 sts once, 2 sts 1 (1, 2, 2) time(s), then dec 1 st every row 4 (4, 3, 3) times—16 (17, 18, 19) sts rem. When piece is same length as back to shoulder, BO at shoulder edge every other row 5 (5, 6, 6) sts, 5 (6, 6, 6) sts, then 6 (6, 6, 7) sts.

RIGHT FRONT

Work as for left front, reversing shaping: work side seam decs 3 sts from end of designated RS rows as k2tog, k1 and *at the same time* make buttonholes on band, spacing as for buttons on left band. Mark placement of buttons on left band; lowest button is about

6" (15 cm) from lower edge and top button is just below first inc for lapel; space third button evenly between. *Buttonhole:* Work 4 sts from RS edge, BO 1 st, complete row. On the next row, CO 1 new st over gap.

SLEEVES

CO 40 (41, 42, 43) sts.

ROW 1: (RS) K1, work Jacket chart to last st, k1.

Cont in patt, keeping first and last sts of each row in garter st, until piece measures 2 (3½, 1½, ¾)" (5 [8, 4, 2] cm), ending after a WS row.

NEXT ROW: (RS; inc row) K1, M1, work in patt to last st, M1, k1—2 sts inc'd.

Cont in patt, working inc sts into patt and *at the same time* rep inc row every 2 (1½, 1½, 1½)" (5 [4, 4, 4] cm) 7 (8, 9, 10) more times—56 (59, 62, 65) sts.

Cont in patt until sleeve measures 17" (43 cm) or desired length to sleeve cap.

SHAPE SLEEVE CAP

BO 3 sts at beg of next 2 (2, 2, 4) rows, BO 2 sts at beg of next 4 (4, 6, 2) rows, BO 1 st at beg of next 16 (16, 12, 12) rows, BO 2 sts at beg of next 6 (4, 4, 6) rows, BO 3 sts at beg of next 2 (4, 2, 2) rows, BO 4 sts at beg of next (0, 0, 2, 2) rows, BO rem 8 (9, 10, 11) sts.

FINISHING AND COLLAR

With yarn threaded on a tapestry needle, sew shoulder seams.

With WS facing, pick up and knit 69 (69, 73, 73) sts along back neck edge between lapels. Work in patt following chart and keeping first and last st of every row in garter st. Work until collar measures ⅜" (1 cm) from picked-up edge. Inc 2 sts at each shoulder on next row, then again at 1½" (4 cm) and *at the same time* at ⅜" (1 cm) inc 1 st at front edge, then again at 1½" (4 cm) and 2½" (6 cm) working all new sts into patt. Work until collar measures 2¾" (7 cm) from picked-up row. BO all sts.

Sew in sleeves, then sew underarm and side seams. With RS facing, work 1 row of shrimp st (see Glossary) beg at left front upper edge down left front, along lower edge, and up right front ending at upper edge. Fold collar and lapel down; this will be the RS when worn. Work 1 row of shrimp st along left front lapel, along collar edge and along right front lapel. With RS facing, work 1 row of shrimp st at lower edges of sleeves.

With sewing needle and thread, sew buttons along left front band to correspond with buttonholes. Weave in ends.

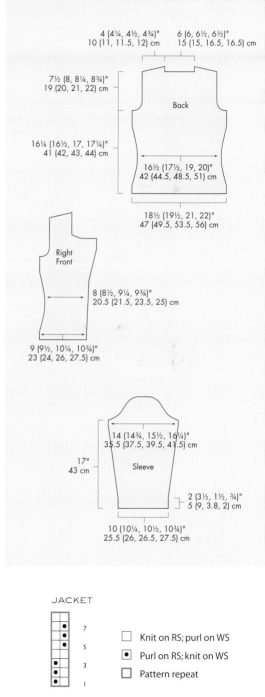

4 (4¼, 4½, 4¾)"
10 (11, 11.5, 12) cm

6 (6, 6½, 6½)"
15 (15, 16.5, 16.5) cm

7½ (8, 8¼, 8¾)"
19 (20, 21, 22) cm

Back

16¼ (16½, 17, 17¼)"
41 (42, 43, 44) cm

16½ (17½, 19, 20)"
42 (44.5, 48.5, 51) cm

18½ (19½, 21, 22)"
47 (49.5, 53.5, 56) cm

Right Front

8 (8½, 9¼, 9¾)"
20.5 (21.5, 23.5, 25) cm

9 (9½, 10¼, 10¾)"
23 (24, 26, 27.5) cm

14 (14¾, 15½, 16¼)"
35.5 (37.5, 39.5, 41.5) cm

17"
43 cm

Sleeve

2 (3½, 1½, ¾)"
5 (9, 3.8, 2) cm

10 (10¼, 10½, 10¾)"
25.5 (26, 26.5, 27.5) cm

JACKET

	7
	5
	3
	1

☐ Knit on RS; purl on WS

⊡ Purl on RS; knit on WS

☐ Pattern repeat

abbreviations

BEG(S)	begin(s); beginning
BO	bind off
CC	contrasting color
CM	centimeter(s)
CN	cable needle
CO	cast on
CONT	continue(s); continuing
DEC(S)	decrease(s); decreasing
DPN	double-pointed needles
FOLL	follow(s); following
G	gram(s)
INC(S)	increase(s); increasing
K	knit
K1F&B	knit into the front and back of same stitch
KWISE	knitwise, as if to knit
M	marker(s)
MC	main color
MM	millimeter(s)
M1	make one (increase)
NDL	needle
P1F&B	purl into front and back of same stitch
PATT(S)	pattern(s)
PSSO	pass slipped stitch over
PWISE	purlwise, as if to purl
REM	remain(s); remaining
REP	repeat(s); repeating
REV ST ST	reverse stockinette stitch
RND(S)	round(s)

RS	right side
SL	slip
SL ST	slip st (slip 1 stitch purlwise unless otherwise indicated)
SSK	slip 2 stitches knitwise, one at a time, from the left needle to right needle, insert left needle tip through both front loops and knit together from this position (1 stitch decrease)
ST(S)	stitch(es)
ST ST	stockinette stitch
TBL	through back loop
TOG	together
WS	wrong side
WYB	with yarn in back
WYF	with yarn in front
YD	yard(s)
YO	yarnover
*	repeat starting point
* *	repeat all instructions between asterisks
( )	alternate measurements and/or instructions
[ ]	work instructions as a group

glossary

BIND-OFFS

THREE-NEEDLE BIND-OFF

Place the stitches to be joined onto two separate needles and hold the needles parallel so that the right sides of knitting face together. Insert a third needle into the first stitch on each of two needles (FIGURE 1) and knit them together as one stitch (FIGURE 2), *knit the next stitch on each needle the same way, then use the left needle tip to lift the first stitch over the second and off the needle (FIGURE 3). Repeat from * until no stitches remain on first two needles. Cut yarn and pull tail through last stitch to secure.

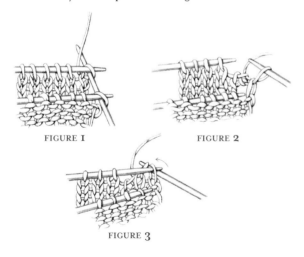

FIGURE 1   FIGURE 2

FIGURE 3

CAST-ONS

BACKWARD-LOOP CAST-ON

*Loop working yarn and place it on needle backward so that it doesn't unwind. Repeat from *.

CABLE CAST-ON

If there are no stitches on the needles, make a slipknot of working yarn and place it on the needle, then use the knitted method to cast-on one more stitch—two stitches on needle. Hold needle with working yarn in your left hand with the wrong side of the work facing you. *Insert right needle *between* the first two stitches on left needle (FIGURE 1), wrap yarn around needle as if to knit, draw yarn through (FIGURE 2), and place new loop on left needle (FIGURE 3) to form a new stitch. Repeat from * for the desired number of stitches, always working between the first two stitches on the left needle.

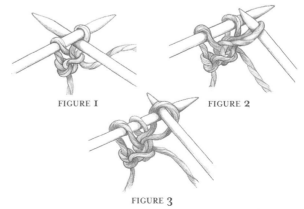

FIGURE 1   FIGURE 2

FIGURE 3

CROCHET

CROCHET CHAIN (CH)

Make a slipknot and place it on crochet hook if there isn't a loop already on the hook. *Yarn over hook and draw through loop on hook. Repeat from *. To fasten off, cut yarn and draw end through last loop formed.

DOUBLE CROCHET (DC)

*Yarn over hook, insert hook into a stitch, yarn over hook (FIGURE 1) and draw a loop through (three loops on hook), yarn over hook and draw a loop through two loops (FIGURE 2), yarn over hook and draw it through the remaining two loops (FIGURE 3). Repeat from *.

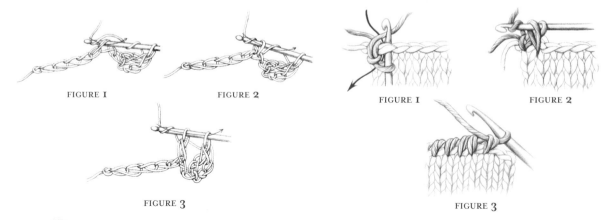

FIGURE I   FIGURE 2

FIGURE 3

HALF DOUBLE CROCHET (HDC)

*Yarn over hook, insert hook into a stitch, yarn over hook and draw a loop through (three loops on hook), yarn over hook (FIGURE 1) and draw a loop through all the loops on the hook (FIGURE 2). Repeat from *.

FIGURE I   FIGURE 2

REVERSE SINGLE CROCHET (OR SHRIMP STITCH)

Working from left to right, insert hook into a stitch, draw through a loop, bring yarn over hook, and draw it through the first loop. *Insert hook into next stitch to the right (FIGURE 1), draw through a loop, bring yarn over hook again (FIGURE 2), and draw a loop through both loops on hook (Figure 3). Repeat from *.

FIGURE I   FIGURE 2

FIGURE 3

SINGLE CROCHET (SC)

*Insert hook into the second chain from the hook (or the next stitch), yarn over hook and draw through a loop, yarn over hook (FIGURE 1), and draw it through both loops on hook (FIGURE 2). Repeat from *.

FIGURE 1   FIGURE 2

SC2TOG DECREASE (SC2TOG)

Insert hook in next stitch, yarn over hook and draw a loop through the stitch (two loops on hook; FIGURE 1), insert hook in next stitch, yarn over hook and draw a loop through this stitch (three loops on hook), yarn over hook (FIGURE 2) and draw a loop through all three loops on hook (FIGURE 3).

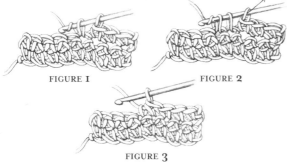

FIGURE 1   FIGURE 2

FIGURE 3

SLIP-STITCH CROCHET (SL ST)

*Insert hook into stitch, yarn over hook and draw a loop through both the stitch and the loop already on hook. Repeat from *.

TREBLE CROCHET (TR)

*Wrap yarn around hook two times, insert hook into a stitch, yarn over hook and draw a loop through (four loops on hook; (FIGURE 1), yarn over hook and draw a loop through two loops (FIGURE 2), yarn over hook and draw a loop through the next two loops, yarn over hook and draw it through the remaining two loops (FIGURE 3). Repeat from *.

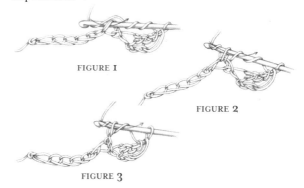

FIGURE 1

FIGURE 2

FIGURE 3

DOUBLE TREBLE CROCHET (DTR)

*Wrap yarn around hook three times, insert hook into stitch, yarn over hook and draw up a loop (five loops on hook), [yarn over hook and draw it through two loops] four times. Repeat from *.

EMBROIDERY

CHAIN STITCH

Bring threaded needle out from back to front at center of a knitted stitch. Form a short loop and insert needle back where it came out. Keeping the loop under the needle, bring needle back out in center of next stitch to the right.

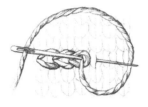

DAISY STITCH

*Bring threaded needle out of knitted background from back to front, form a short loop and insert needle into background where it came out. Keeping the loop under the needle, bring the needle back out of the background a short distance away (FIGURE 1), pull loop snug, and insert needle into fabric on far side of loop. Beginning each stitch at the same point in the background, repeat from * for the desired number of petals (FIGURE 2; six petals shown).

FIGURE 1

FIGURE 2

FRENCH KNOT

Bring threaded needle out of knitted background from back to front, wrap yarn around needle one to three times, and use your thumb to hold the wraps in place while you insert needle into background a short distance from where it came out. Pull the needle through the wraps into the background.

I-CORD

Using two double-pointed needles, cast on the desired number of stitches (usually three to four). *Without turning the needle, slide stitches to other end of needle, pull the yarn around the back, and knit the stitches as usual. Repeat from * for desired length.

INCREASES

RAISED MAKE ONE—LEFT SLANT (M1L)

Note: Use the left slant if no direction of slant is specified. With left needle tip, lift the strand between the last knitted stitch and the first stitch on the left needle from front to back (FIGURE 1), then knit the lifted loop through the back (FIGURE 2).

FIGURE 1

FIGURE 2

PICK UP & KNIT

PICK UP & KNIT ALONG CO OR BO EDGE

With right side facing and working from right to left, insert the tip of the needle into the center of the stitch below the bind-off or cast-on edge (FIGURE 1), wrap yarn around needle, and pull through a loop (FIGURE 2). Pick up one stitch for every existing stitch.

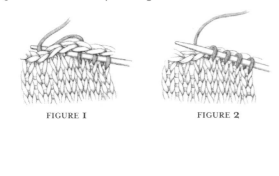

FIGURE 1   FIGURE 2

PICK UP AND KNIT ALONG SHAPED EDGE

With right side facing and working from right to left, insert tip of needle between last and second-to-last stitches, wrap yarn around needle, and pull through a loop. Pick up and knit about three stitches for every four rows, adjusting as necessary so that picked-up edge lays flat.

POMPON

Cut two circles of cardboard, each ½"(1.3 cm) larger than desired finished pompon width. Cut a small circle out of the center and a small wedge out of the side of each circle (FIGURE 1). Tie a strand of yarn between the circles, hold circles together and wrap with yarn—the more wraps, the thicker the pompon. Cut between the circles and knot the tie strand tightly (FIGURE 2). Place pompon between two smaller cardboard circles held together with a needle and trim the edges (FIGURE 3). This technique comes from *Nicky Epstein's Knitted Embellishments,* Interweave, 1999.

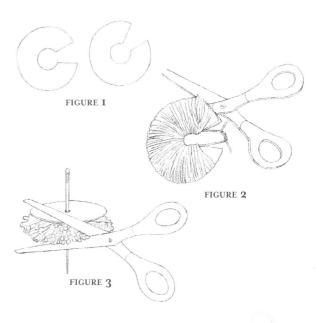

FIGURE 1

FIGURE 2

FIGURE 3

SEAMS

BACKSTITCH SEAM—HORIZONTAL

Pin pieces to be seamed with right sides facing together. Working from right to left just below the edge, bring threaded needle up between the first two stitches on each piece of knitted fabric, then back down through both layers, one stitch to the right of the starting point (FIGURE 1). *Bring the needle up through both layers a stitch to the left of the backstitch just made (FIGURE 2), then back down to the right, through the same hole used before (FIGURE 3). Repeat from *, working backward one stitch for every two stitches worked forward.

INVISIBLE HORIZONTAL SEAM

Working with the bound-off edges opposite each other, right sides of the knitting facing you, and working into the stitches just below the bound-off edges, bring threaded tapestry needle out at the center of the first stitch (i.e., go under half of the first stitch) on one side of the seam, then bring needle in and out under the first whole stitch on the other side (FIGURE 1). *Bring needle into the center of the same stitch it came out of before, then out in the center of the adjacent stitch (FIGURE 2). Bring needle in and out under the next whole stitch on the other side (FIGURE 3). Repeat from *, ending with a half-stitch on the first side.

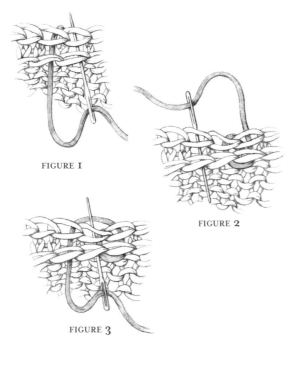

FIGURE 1

FIGURE 2

FIGURE 3

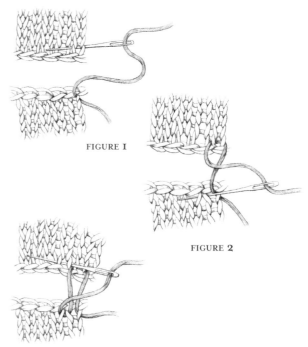

FIGURE 1

FIGURE 2

FIGURE 3

INVISIBLE VERTICAL TO HORIZONTAL SEAM

With yarn threaded on a tapestry needle, pick up one bar between the first two stitches along the vertical edge (Figure 1), then pick up one complete stitch along the horizontal edge (Figure 2). *Pick up the next one or two bars on the first piece, then the next whole stitch on the other piece (Figure 3). Repeat from *, ending by picking up one bar on the vertical edge.

INVISIBLE VERTICAL SEAM (OR MATTRESS STITCH)

Place the pieces to be seamed on a table, right sides facing up. Begin at the lower edge and work upward as follows: Insert threaded needle under one bar between the two edge stitches on one piece, then under the corresponding bar plus the bar above it on the other piece (Figure 1). *Pick up the next two bars on the first piece (Figure 2), then the next two bars on the other (Figure 3). Repeat from *, ending by picking up the last bar or pair of bars on the first piece.

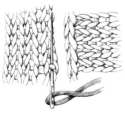

FIGURE 1

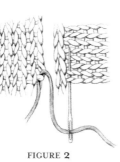

FIGURE 2

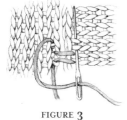

FIGURE 3

FIGURE 1

FIGURE 2

FIGURE 3

yarns

COATS HP

The following Coats yarns are not currently distributed in the United States. See below for substitutions. hpgruppen.dk

Fonty Kidopale; Fonty Ombelle; Løve Haekle-garn; Løve Cosy; Løve Iceland; Løve Kick; Løve Lima; Løve Lino; Løve Opera; Løve Ragsokgarn; Løve Rustico; Løve Siesta; Løve Zeta

SANDNESGARN

Distributed in the United States by Swedish Yarn, Inc., PO Box 2069, Jamestown, NC 27282; swedishyarn.com

Alpakka; Sisu; Fritidsgarn; Peer Gynt

YARN SUBSTITUTIONS

Since the original publication of this book in Denmark, a number of the yarns used have been discontinued or become unavailable through United States distributors. I suggest substituting the following yarns, but make sure to work a gauge swatch and make adjustments as needed. Be sure to purchase enough yards of substitute yarns, as they may be available in a different put-up than the original. Substitute yarns may have a different fiber content and more or less yardage for the same weight.

For *Cosy* (100% superwash wool; 137 yd [125 m]/100 g), try *Rowan Scottish Tweed Chunky* (100% wool; 109 yd [100 m]/100 g).

For *Haeklegarn*, substitute any no. 5 crochet cotton.

For *Iceland* (50% wool, 35% acrylic, 15% alpaca; 165 yd (150 m)/50 g), try *Rowan Scottish Tweed DK* (100% wool, 123 yd [112 m]/50 g).

For *Kick* (50% cotton, 50% acrylic; 165 yd [150 m]/50 g), try *Rowan 4-ply Cotton* (100% cotton, 185 yd [160 m]/50 g).

For *Kidopale* (70% kid mohair, 30% polyamide; 275 yd [250 m]/25 g), try *Rowan Kidsilk Haze* (70% kid mohair, 30% silk; 229 yd [206 m]/25 g).

For *Lima* (38% linen, 31% cotton, 31% viscose; 223 yd [104 m]/50 g), try *Louet Euroflax Paris* (100% linen; 580 yd [530 m]/100 g) or no. 8 crochet cotton.

For *Lino* (63% cotton, 37% linen; 76 yd [70 m]/50 g), try *Garnstudio Bomull-Lin* (53% cotton, 47% linen; 93 yd [85 m]/50 g).

For *Ombelle* (70% mohair, 25% wool, 5% polyamid; 159 yd [145 m]/50 g), try 2 strands of *Rowan Kidsilk Haze* held double.

For *Opera* (86% wool, 9% viscose, 5% polyester; 128 yd [117 m]/50 g), try *Rowan Cashsoft DK* (57% Merino wool, 33% microfiber, 10% cashmere; 142 yd [130 m]/50 g) plus a thin Lurex thread.

For *Ragsokgarn* (70% superwash wool, 30% nylon; 88 yd [80 m]/50 g), try *Garnstudio Alaska* (100% wool; 82 yd [75 m]/50 g).

For *Løve Rustico* (55% acrylic, 45% cotton; 109 yd [100 m]/50 g), try *Rowan Summer Tweed* (70% wool, 30% silk; 118 yd [108 m]/50 g) or *GGH Silky Tweed* (55% wool, 25% silk, 20% microfiber; 137 yd [125 m]/50 g).

For *Siesta* (50% viscose, 50% acrylic; 126 yd [115 m]/50 g), try *Dale Svale* (50% cotton, 40% rayon, 10% silk; 114 yd [104 m]/50 g) or *GGH Mystik* (54% cotton, 46% viscose; 121 yd [111 m]/50 g).

For *Zeta* (100% silk; 104 yd [95 m]/50 g), try *GGH Leona* (50% cotton, 50% acrylic; 104 yd [95 m]/50 g) or *GGH Cadiz Unito* (51% cotton, 33% acrylic, 16% rayon; 104 yd [95 m]/50 g).

index

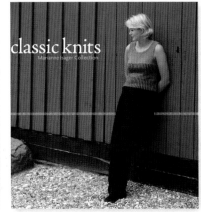